Working Papers: Chapters

Accounting, 27e

Carl S. Warren
Professor Emeritus of Accounting
University of Georgia, Athens

James M. Reeve
Professor Emeritus of Accounting
University of Tennessee, Knoxville

Jonathan E. Duchac
Professor of Accounting
Wake Forest University

Australia • Brazil • Mexico • Singapore • United Kingdom • United States

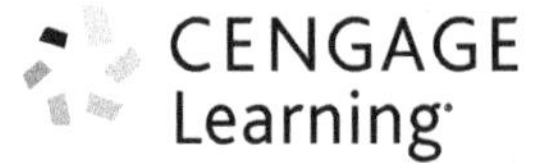

© 2018, 2016 Cengage Learning

ALL RIGHTS RESERVED. No part of this work covered by the copyright herein may be reproduced, transmitted, stored, or used in any form or by any means graphic, electronic, or mechanical, including but not limited to photocopying, recording, scanning, digitizing, taping, Web distribution, information networks, or information storage and retrieval systems, except as permitted under Section 107 or 108 of the 1976 United States Copyright Act, without the prior written permission of the publisher.

For product information and technology assistance, contact us at **Cengage Learning Customer & Sales Support, 1-800-354-9706**.

For permission to use material from this text or product, submit all requests online at **www.cengage.com/permissions**
Further permissions questions can be emailed to **permissionrequest@cengage.com**.

ISBN: 978-1-337-27216-2

Cengage Learning
20 Channel Center Street
Boston, MA 02210
USA

Cengage Learning is a leading provider of customized learning solutions with office locations around the globe, including Singapore, the United Kingdom, Australia, Mexico, Brazil, and Japan. Locate your local office at: **www.cengage.com/global**.

Cengage Learning products are represented in Canada by Nelson Education, Ltd.

To learn more about Cengage Learning Solutions, visit **www.cengage.com**.

Purchase any of our products at your local college store or at our preferred online store **www.cengagebrain.com**.

Printed in the United States of America
1 2 3 4 5 22 21 20 19 18

CONTENTS

18	Introduction to Managerial Accounting	759
19	Job Order Costing	783
20	Process Cost Systems	813
21	Cost-Volume-Profit Analysis	875
22	Budgeting	917
23	Evaluating Variances from Standard Costs	959
24	Decentralized Operations	1023
25	Differential Analysis, Product Pricing, and Activity-Based Costing	1071
26	Capital Investment Analysis	1115

PREFACE

The working papers include problem-specific forms for preparing solutions for Exercises, A&B Problems, the Continuing Problem, and the Comprehensive Problems from the textbook. These forms, with preprinted headings, provide a structure for the problems, which will help you get started and save you time.

Based on students' testimonials and instructors' feedback, the forms in the working papers have been streamlined to make them simpler to use and to better reflect the changing environment of business. For example, the vertical rules that separated digits of numbers entered into journals, ledgers, and statements have been removed, making it easier to write in numbers.

Note that when entering whole amounts into the forms, your instructor will direct you on whether to include a decimal point and zeroes (e.g., 100.00) or to omit those (e.g., 100).

EXERCISE 18-1

a. Wheels: ______________________

b. Glass used in the vehicle's windshield: ______________________

c. Wages of assembly line worker: ______________________

d. V8 automobile engine: ______________________

e. Depreciation of robotic assembly line equipment: ______________________

f. Steering wheel: ______________________

g. Painting safety masks for employees working in the paint room: ______________________

h. Salary of test driver: ______________________

EXERCISE 18-2

a. Resins for body wash products: ______________________

b. Scents and fragrances used in making soaps and detergents: ______________________

c. Plant manager salary for the Iowa City, Iowa, plant: ______________________

d. Depreciation on the Auburn, Maine, manufacturing plant: ______________________

e. Depreciation on assembly line in the Mehoopany, Pennsylvania, paper products plant: ______________________

f. Maintenance supplies: ______________________

g. Packaging materials, which are a significant portion of the total product cost: ______________________

h. Wages of production line employees at the Pineville, Louisiana, soap and detergent plant: ______________________

i. Wages paid to Packaging Department employees in the Bear River City, Utah, paper products plant: ______________________

j. Salary of process engineers: ______________________

© 2018 Cengage. May not be scanned, copied or duplicated, or posted to a publicly accessible website, in whole or in part.

EXERCISE 18-3

a. Plant manager's salary at Buffalo, New York, stamping plant, which manufactures auto and truck subassemblies: ______________________

b. Depreciation on Flat Rock, Michigan, assembly plant: ______________________

c. Dividends paid to shareholders: ______________________

d. Machine lubricant used to maintain the assembly line at the Louisville, Kentucky, assembly plant: ______________________

e. Leather to be used in vehicles that have leather interiors: ______________________

f. Depreciation on mechanical robots used on the assembly line: ______________________

g. Consultant fees for a study of production line efficiency: ______________________

h. Dealership sales incentives: ______________________

i. Vice president of human resources' salary: ______________________

j. Property taxes on the Detroit, Michigan, headquarters building: ______________________

EXERCISE 18-4

a. Cost of information technology support for the corporate headquarters: ______________________

b. Depreciation on sewing machines: ______________________

c. Fabric used during production: ______________________

d. Depreciation on office equipment: ______________________

e. Advertising expenses: ______________________

f. Repairs and maintenance costs for sewing machines: ______________________

g. Salary of production quality control supervisor: ______________________

h. Utility costs for office building: ______________________

i. Sales commissions: ______________________

j. Salaries of distribution center personnel: ______________________

k. Wages of sewing machine operators: ______________________

l. Factory janitorial supplies: ______________________

m. Chief financial officer's salary: ______________________

n. Travel costs of media relations employees: ______________________

o. Factory supervisors' salaries: ______________________

p. Oil used to lubricate sewing machines: ______________________

q. Property taxes on factory building and equipment: ______________________

© 2018 Cengage. May not be scanned, copied or duplicated, or posted to a publicly accessible website, in whole or in part.

EXERCISE 18-5

a. ______________________________

b. ______________________________

c. ______________________________

d. ______________________________

e. ______________________________

f. ______________________________

g. ______________________________

EXERCISE 18-6

a. ______________________________

b. ______________________________

c. ______________________________

d. ______________________________

e. ______________________________

f. ______________________________

g. ______________________________

EXERCISE 18-7

a. Cost to lease (rent) railroad cars: ______________________________

b. Cost of track and bed (ballast) replacement: ______________________________

c. Diesel fuel costs: ______________________________

d. Cost to lease (rent) train locomotives: ______________________________

e. Depreciation of terminal facilities: ______________________________

f. Maintenance costs of right-of-way, bridges, and buildings: ______________________________

g. Salaries of dispatching and communications personnel: ______________________________

h. Headquarters information technology support staff salaries: ______________________________

i. Safety training costs: ______________________________

j. Wages of train engineers: ______________________________

k. Wages of switch and classification yard personnel: ______________________________

l. Costs of accident cleanup: ______________________________

© 2018 Cengage. May not be scanned, copied or duplicated, or posted to a publicly accessible website, in whole or in part.

EXERCISE 18-8

1. Energy Efficiency: ______________________

2. Fuel Efficiency: ______________________

3. Material Use Efficiency: ______________________

4. Waste Efficiency: ______________________

EXERCISE 18-9

1. ______________________

2. ______________________

Manufacturing Costs

© 2018 Cengage. May not be scanned, copied or duplicated, or posted to a publicly accessible website, in whole or in part.

EXERCISE 18-10

a.

Income Statement

b. Inventory balances on January 31:

Materials: ______________________

Work in Process: ______________________

Finished Goods: ______________________

© 2018 Cengage. May not be scanned, copied or duplicated, or posted to a publicly accessible website, in whole or in part.

EXERCISE 18-11

Balance Sheet

EXERCISE 18-12

© 2018 Cengage. May not be scanned, copied or duplicated, or posted to a publicly accessible website, in whole or in part.

EXERCISE 18-13

Work in process inventory, August 1	$ 19,660	$ 41,650	(e) ________
Total manufacturing costs incurred during August	332,750	(c) ________	1,075,000
Total manufacturing costs	(a) ________	$515,770	$1,240,000
Work in process inventory, August 31	23,500	54,000	(f) ________
Cost of goods manufactured	(b) ________	(d) ________	$1,068,000

EXERCISE 18-14

EXERCISE 18-15

Finished goods inventory, June 1	$116,600	$ 38,880	(e) ________
Cost of goods manufactured	825,900	(c) ________	180,000
Cost of finished goods available for sale	(a) ________	$540,000	$1,100,000
Finished goods inventory, June 30	130,000	70,000	(f) ________
Cost of goods sold	(b) ________	(d) ________	$ 945,000

© 2018 Cengage. May not be scanned, copied or duplicated, or posted to a publicly accessible website, in whole or in part.

EXERCISE 18-16

a.

Statement of Cost of Goods Manufactured

© 2018 Cengage. May not be scanned, copied or duplicated, or posted to a publicly accessible website, in whole or in part.

EXERCISE 18-16, Concluded

b.

EXERCISE 18-17

a., b., and c.

© 2018 Cengage. May not be scanned, copied or duplicated, or posted to a publicly accessible website, in whole or in part.

EXERCISE 18-18

a. through e.

EXERCISE 18-19

© 2018 Cengage. May not be scanned, copied or duplicated, or posted to a publicly accessible website, in whole or in part.

This Page Not Used.

© 2018 Cengage. May not be scanned, copied or duplicated, or posted to a publicly accessible website, in whole or in part.

PROBLEM 18-1 ___

Cost	Product Costs			Period Costs	
	Direct Materials Cost	Direct Labor Cost	Factory Overhead Cost	Selling Expense	Administrative Expense
a.					
b.					
c.					
d.					
e.					
f.					
g.					
h.					
i.					
j.					
k.					
l.					
m.					
n.					
o.					
p.					
q.					
r.					
s.					
t.					
u.					
v.					
w.					
x.					
y.					
z.					

© 2018 Cengage. May not be scanned, copied or duplicated, or posted to a publicly accessible website, in whole or in part.

This Page Not Used.

© 2018 Cengage. May not be scanned, copied or duplicated, or posted to a publicly accessible website, in whole or in part.

PROBLEM 18-2 ___

Cost	Product Costs			Period Costs	
	Direct Materials Cost	Direct Labor Cost	Factory Overhead Cost	Selling Expense	Administrative Expense
a.					
b.					
c.					
d.					
e.					
f.					
g.					
h.					
i.					
j.					
k.					
l.					
m.					
n.					
o.					
p.					
q.					
r.					
s.					
t.					
u.					
v.					
w.					
x.					

© 2018 Cengage. May not be scanned, copied or duplicated, or posted to a publicly accessible website, in whole or in part.

This Page Not Used.

© 2018 Cengage. May not be scanned, copied or duplicated, or posted to a publicly accessible website, in whole or in part.

Name ______________________________

PROBLEM 18-3 ___

1. ____

____

____

____

____

2.

Cost	Direct	Indirect
a.		
b.		
c.		
d.		
e.		
f.		
g.		
h.		
i.		
j.		
k.		
l.		
m.		
n.		
o.		
p.		
q.		
r.		
s.		
t.		
u.		
v.		
w.		

© 2018 Cengage. May not be scanned, copied or duplicated, or posted to a publicly accessible website, in whole or in part.

This Page Not Used.

© 2018 Cengage. May not be scanned, copied or duplicated, or posted to a publicly accessible website, in whole or in part.

PROBLEM 18-4 ___

1. ________________ Company

   a. ______________________________
   b. ______________________________
   c. ______________________________
   d. ______________________________
   e. ______________________________
   f. ______________________________

   ________________ Company

   a. ______________________________
   b. ______________________________
   c. ______________________________
   d. ______________________________
   e. ______________________________
   f. ______________________________

© 2018 Cengage. May not be scanned, copied or duplicated, or posted to a publicly accessible website, in whole or in part.

PROBLEM 18-4 ___, Continued

2.

Statement of Cost of Goods Manufactured

© 2018 Cengage. May not be scanned, copied or duplicated, or posted to a publicly accessible website, in whole or in part.

PROBLEM 18-4 ___, Concluded

3.

Income Statement

© 2018 Cengage. May not be scanned, copied or duplicated, or posted to a publicly accessible website, in whole or in part.

This Page Not Used.

© 2018 Cengage. May not be scanned, copied or duplicated, or posted to a publicly accessible website, in whole or in part.

PROBLEM 18-5 ___

1.

Statement of Cost of Goods Manufactured

© 2018 Cengage. May not be scanned, copied or duplicated, or posted to a publicly accessible website, in whole or in part.

PROBLEM 18-5 ___, Concluded

2.

Income Statement

© 2018 Cengage. May not be scanned, copied or duplicated, or posted to a publicly accessible website, in whole or in part.

EXERCISE 19-1

a. ______________________

b. ______________________

c. ______________________

d. ______________________

e. ______________________

EXERCISE 19-2

a.

RECEIVED			ISSUED			BALANCE			
Receiving Report Number	Quantity	Unit Price	Materials Requisition Number	Quantity	Amount	Date	Quantity	Unit Price	Amount
						May 1	285	$30.00	$8,550
40	130	$32.00				May 4	______	______	______
							______	______	______
			91	365	______	May 10	______	______	______
44	110	38.00				May 21	______	______	______
							______	______	______
			97	100	______	May 27	______	______	______

b. ______________________

____

c.

JOURNAL PAGE

	DATE		DESCRIPTION	POST. REF.	DEBIT	CREDIT	
1							1
2							2
3							3
4							4

d. ______________________

____

____

____

____

____

____

© 2018 Cengage. May not be scanned, copied or duplicated, or posted to a publicly accessible website, in whole or in part.

EXERCISE 19-3

JOURNAL

PAGE

	DATE		DESCRIPTION	POST. REF.	DEBIT	CREDIT	
1							1
2							2
3							3
4							4

EXERCISE 19-4

a. and b.

JOURNAL

PAGE

	DATE		DESCRIPTION	POST. REF.	DEBIT	CREDIT	
1							1
2							2
3							3
4							4
5							5
6							6
7							7
8							8
9							9
10							10
11							11
12							12

c.

	Fabric	Polyester Filling	Lumber	Glue

© 2018 Cengage. May not be scanned, copied or duplicated, or posted to a publicly accessible website, in whole or in part.

EXERCISE 19-5

JOURNAL

PAGE

	DATE		DESCRIPTION	POST. REF.	DEBIT	CREDIT	
1							1
2							2
3							3
4							4

EXERCISE 19-6

a.

JOURNAL

PAGE

	DATE		DESCRIPTION	POST. REF.	DEBIT	CREDIT	
1							1
2							2
3							3
4							4

Supporting calculations:

b.

© 2018 Cengage. May not be scanned, copied or duplicated, or posted to a publicly accessible website, in whole or in part.

EXERCISE 19-7

a. and b.

JOURNAL PAGE

	DATE		DESCRIPTION	POST. REF.	DEBIT	CREDIT	
1							1
2							2
3							3
4							4
5							5
6							6
7							7
8							8
9							9
10							10
11							11
12							12

EXERCISE 19-8

a. Factory 1: ____________________

____

b. Factory 2: ____________________

____

c.

JOURNAL PAGE

	DATE		DESCRIPTION	POST. REF.	DEBIT	CREDIT	
1							1
2							2
3							3
4							4
5							5
6							6
7							7
8							8
9							9

© 2018 Cengage. May not be scanned, copied or duplicated, or posted to a publicly accessible website, in whole or in part.

EXERCISE 19-8, Concluded

d. Factory 1: ____________________

Factory 2: ____________________

EXERCISE 19-9

© 2018 Cengage. May not be scanned, copied or duplicated, or posted to a publicly accessible website, in whole or in part.

EXERCISE 19-10

a.

b.

c.

d.

© 2018 Cengage. May not be scanned, copied or duplicated, or posted to a publicly accessible website, in whole or in part.

EXERCISE 19-11

a.

JOURNAL PAGE

	DATE		DESCRIPTION	POST. REF.	DEBIT	CREDIT	
1							1
2							2
3							3
4							4

b.

© 2018 Cengage. May not be scanned, copied or duplicated, or posted to a publicly accessible website, in whole or in part.

EXERCISE 19-12

a. through d.

JOURNAL

PAGE

DATE		DESCRIPTION	POST. REF.	DEBIT	CREDIT

© 2018 Cengage. May not be scanned, copied or duplicated, or posted to a publicly accessible website, in whole or in part.

EXERCISE 19-13

a.

Income Statement

b. Materials inventory:

Work in process inventory:

Finished goods inventory:

© 2018 Cengage. May not be scanned, copied or duplicated, or posted to a publicly accessible website, in whole or in part.

EXERCISE 19-14

a.

Date	Job No.	Quantity	Product	Amount	Unit Cost
Jan. 2	1	520	TT	$16,120	________
Jan. 15	22	1,610	SS	20,125	________
Feb. 3	30	1,420	SS	25,560	________
Mar. 7	41	670	TT	15,075	________
Mar. 24	49	2,210	SLK	22,100	________
May 19	58	2,550	SLK	31,875	________
June 12	65	620	TT	10,540	________
Aug. 18	78	3,110	SLK	48,205	________
Sept. 2	82	1,210	SS	16,940	________
Nov. 14	92	750	TT	8,250	________
Dec. 12	98	2,700	SLK	52,650	________

Unit Costs for TT

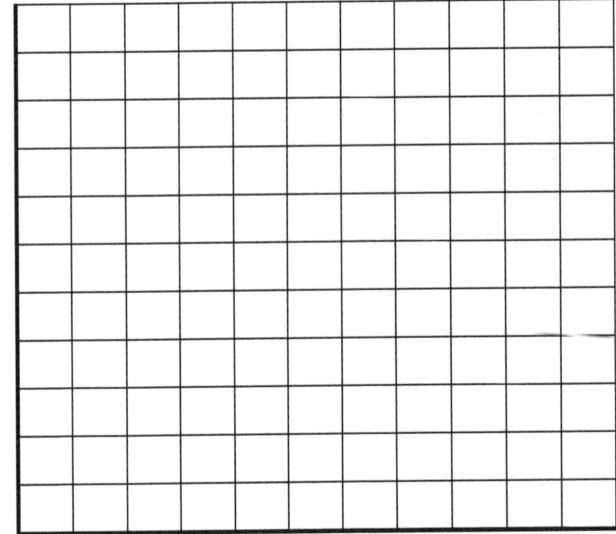

© 2018 Cengage. May not be scanned, copied or duplicated, or posted to a publicly accessible website, in whole or in part.

EXERCISE 19-14, Continued

Unit Costs for SS

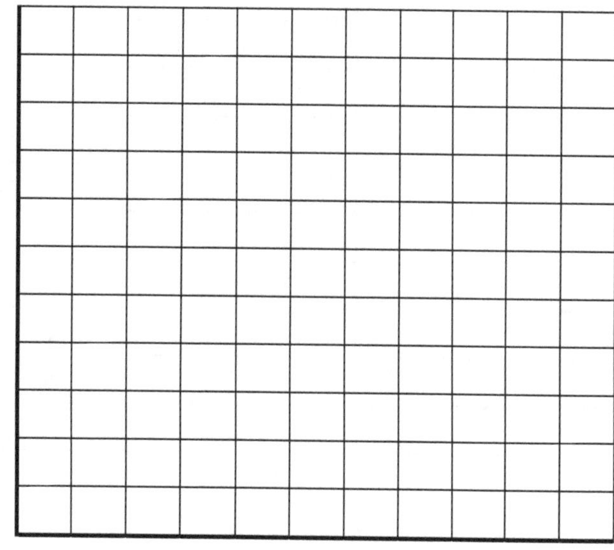

Job Number

Unit Costs for SLK

Unit Cost

Job Number

© 2018 Cengage. May not be scanned, copied or duplicated, or posted to a publicly accessible website, in whole or in part.

EXERCISE 19-14, Concluded

b. ______________________________

© 2018 Cengage. May not be scanned, copied or duplicated, or posted to a publicly accessible website, in whole or in part.

EXERCISE 19-15

a. ______________________

Job 101:

© 2018 Cengage. May not be scanned, copied or duplicated, or posted to a publicly accessible website, in whole or in part.

EXERCISE 19-15, Continued

Job 105:

© 2018 Cengage. May not be scanned, copied or duplicated, or posted to a publicly accessible website, in whole or in part.

EXERCISE 19-15, Concluded

b. ______________________

© 2018 Cengage. May not be scanned, copied or duplicated, or posted to a publicly accessible website, in whole or in part.

EXERCISE 19-16

a.

JOURNAL

PAGE

	DATE		DESCRIPTION	POST. REF.	DEBIT	CREDIT	
1							1
2							2
3							3
4							4
5							5
6							6
7							7
8							8
9							9
10							10
11							11
12							12
13							13
14							14
15							15
16							16
17							17
18							18
19							19
20							20
21							21
22							22
23							23
24							24
25							25
26							26
27							27
28							28
29							29
30							30
31							31
32							32
33							33
34							34
35							35

© 2018 Cengage. May not be scanned, copied or duplicated, or posted to a publicly accessible website, in whole or in part.

EXERCISE 19-16, Concluded

b.

c.

© 2018 Cengage. May not be scanned, copied or duplicated, or posted to a publicly accessible website, in whole or in part.

EXERCISE 19-17

a. through d.

JOURNAL PAGE

	DATE		DESCRIPTION	POST. REF.	DEBIT	CREDIT	
1							1
2							2
3							3
4							4
5							5
6							6
7							7
8							8
9							9
10							10
11							11
12							12

Supporting calculations:

© 2018 Cengage. May not be scanned, copied or duplicated, or posted to a publicly accessible website, in whole or in part.

PROBLEM 19-1 ___

a. through i.

JOURNAL

PAGE

DATE		DESCRIPTION	POST. REF.	DEBIT	CREDIT

© 2018 Cengage. May not be scanned, copied or duplicated, or posted to a publicly accessible website, in whole or in part.

PROBLEM 19-1 ___, Concluded

JOURNAL

PAGE

DATE		DESCRIPTION	POST. REF.	DEBIT	CREDIT

© 2018 Cengage. May not be scanned, copied or duplicated, or posted to a publicly accessible website, in whole or in part.

PROBLEM 19-2 ___

1. a. through g.

JOURNAL

PAGE

DATE		DESCRIPTION	POST. REF.	DEBIT	CREDIT

© 2018 Cengage. May not be scanned, copied or duplicated, or posted to a publicly accessible website, in whole or in part.

PROBLEM 19-2 ___, Continued

f. Computation of cost of jobs finished:

g. Computation of cost of jobs sold:

2.

Work in Process

Finished Goods

© 2018 Cengage. May not be scanned, copied or duplicated, or posted to a publicly accessible website, in whole or in part.

PROBLEM 19-2 ___, Concluded

3.

Schedule of Unfinished Jobs

JOB	DIRECT MATERIALS	DIRECT LABOR	FACTORY OVERHEAD	TOTAL

4.

Schedule of Completed Jobs

JOB	DIRECT MATERIALS	DIRECT LABOR	FACTORY OVERHEAD	TOTAL

© 2018 Cengage. May not be scanned, copied or duplicated, or posted to a publicly accessible website, in whole or in part.

This Page Not Used.

© 2018 Cengage. May not be scanned, copied or duplicated, or posted to a publicly accessible website, in whole or in part.

PROBLEM 19-3 ___

1. and 2.

JOB ORDER COST SHEET

Customer ____________________ Date ____________
Date wanted ____________
Date completed ____________
Job No. ____________

ESTIMATE

Direct Materials	Amount	Direct Labor	Amount	Summary	Amount
____ sq. ft. at $____	____	____ hours at $____	____	Direct materials	____
____ sq. ft. at ____	____	____ hours at ____	____	Direct labor	____
____ sq. ft. at ____	____	____ hours at ____	____	Factory overhead	____
____ sq. ft. at ____	____	____ hours at ____	____		
Total	____	Total	____	Total cost	____

ACTUAL

Mat. Req. No.	Description	Amount	Time Ticket No.	Description	Amount	Item	Amount
____	____	____	____	____	____	Direct materials	____
____	____	____	____	____	____	Direct labor	____
____	____	____	____	____	____	Factory overhead	____
____	____	____	____	____	____		
Total		____	Total		____	Total cost	____

(Direct Materials: Mat. Req. No., Description, Amount; Direct Labor: Time Ticket No., Description, Amount; Summary: Item, Amount)

Comments:

© 2018 Cengage. May not be scanned, copied or duplicated, or posted to a publicly accessible website, in whole or in part.

This Page Not Used.

© 2018 Cengage. May not be scanned, copied or duplicated, or posted to a publicly accessible website, in whole or in part.

PROBLEM 19-4 ___

1. Supporting calculations:

Job No.	Quantity	Work in Process	Direct Materials	Direct Labor	Factory Overhead	Total Cost	Unit Cost	Units Sold	Cost of Goods Sold

(a) ______________________________

____

(b) ______________________________

(c) ______________________________

(d) ______________________________

(e) ______________________________

(f) ______________________________

(g) ______________________________

(h) ______________________________

____

© 2018 Cengage. May not be scanned, copied or duplicated, or posted to a publicly accessible website, in whole or in part.

PROBLEM 19-4 ___, Concluded

2. ____

© 2018 Cengage. May not be scanned, copied or duplicated, or posted to a publicly accessible website, in whole or in part.

PROBLEM 19-5 ___

1.

Income Statement

Supporting calculations:

© 2018 Cengage. May not be scanned, copied or duplicated, or posted to a publicly accessible website, in whole or in part.

PROBLEM 19-5 ___, Concluded

2. ____

© 2018 Cengage. May not be scanned, copied or duplicated, or posted to a publicly accessible website, in whole or in part.

EXERCISE 20-1

a. through e.

JOURNAL

PAGE

	DATE		DESCRIPTION	POST. REF.	DEBIT	CREDIT	
1							1
2							2
3							3
4							4
5							5
6							6
7							7
8							8
9							9
10							10
11							11
12							12
13							13
14							14
15							15
16							16
17							17
18							18
19							19
20							20
21							21
22							22
23							23
24							24
25							25

© 2018 Cengage. May not be scanned, copied or duplicated, or posted to a publicly accessible website, in whole or in part.

Name ______________________________

EXERCISE 20-2

© 2018 Cengage. May not be scanned, copied or duplicated, or posted to a publicly accessible website, in whole or in part.

EXERCISE 20-3

a. and b.

JOURNAL PAGE

	DATE		DESCRIPTION	POST. REF.	DEBIT	CREDIT	
1							1
2							2
3							3
4							4
5							5
6							6
7							7
8							8
9							9
10							10
11							11
12							12
13							13
14							14
15							15
16							16
17							17
18							18
19							19
20							20

© 2018 Cengage. May not be scanned, copied or duplicated, or posted to a publicly accessible website, in whole or in part.

EXERCISE 20-4

a. ____

____

b.

JOURNAL PAGE

	DATE		DESCRIPTION	POST. REF.	DEBIT	CREDIT	
1							1
2							2
3							3
4							4
5							5
6							6
7							7

c. ____

d. ____

EXERCISE 20-5

	A	B	C	D
1			**Equivalent Units**	
2		**Whole Units**	**Direct Materials**	**Conversion**
3				
4				
5				
6				
7				
8				
9				
10				
11				
12				
13				
14				
15				

© 2018 Cengage. May not be scanned, copied or duplicated, or posted to a publicly accessible website, in whole or in part.

EXERCISE 20-6

a. Drawing Department

	A	B	C	D
1			Equivalent Units	
2		Whole Units	Direct Materials	Conversion
3				
4				
5				
6				
7				
8				
9				
10				
11				
12				
13				
14				
15				
16				
17				
18				

b. Winding Department

	A	B	C	D
1			Equivalent Units	
2		Whole Units	Direct Materials	Conversion
3				
4				
5				
6				
7				
8				
9				
10				
11				
12				
13				
14				
15				
16				
17				
18				

© 2018 Cengage. May not be scanned, copied or duplicated, or posted to a publicly accessible website, in whole or in part.

EXERCISE 20-7

a.

b.

	A	B	C	D
1			Equivalent Units	
2		Whole Units	Direct Materials	Conversion
3				
4				
5				
6				
7				
8				
9				
10				
11				
12				
13				
14				
15				
16				
17				
18				

© 2018 Cengage. May not be scanned, copied or duplicated, or posted to a publicly accessible website, in whole or in part.

Name ____________________

EXERCISE 20-8

a. 1. ____________________

2. ____________________

3. ____________________

4. ____________________

5. ____________________

© 2018 Cengage. May not be scanned, copied or duplicated, or posted to a publicly accessible website, in whole or in part.

EXERCISE 20-8, Concluded

b. ____

____

© 2018 Cengage. May not be scanned, copied or duplicated, or posted to a publicly accessible website, in whole or in part.

EXERCISE 20-9

Equivalent units of production:

	CEREAL (IN POUNDS)	BOXES (IN BOXES)	CONVERSION COST (IN BOXES)

Supporting explanation:

© 2018 Cengage. May not be scanned, copied or duplicated, or posted to a publicly accessible website, in whole or in part.

EXERCISE 20-10

a.

b.

c.

© 2018 Cengage. May not be scanned, copied or duplicated, or posted to a publicly accessible website, in whole or in part.

EXERCISE 20-11

a.

b.

	A	B	C	D
1			Equivalent Units	
2		Whole Units	Direct Materials	Conversion
3				
4				
5				
6				
7				
8				
9				
10				
11				
12				
13				
14				
15				
16				

c.

	A	B	C
1		Costs	
2		Direct Materials	Conversion
3			
4			
5			
6			
7			
8			

d. ____

© 2018 Cengage. May not be scanned, copied or duplicated, or posted to a publicly accessible website, in whole or in part.

EXERCISE 20-12

a. 1. ______________________

2.

3. ______________________

4. ______________________

b. ______________________

© 2018 Cengage. May not be scanned, copied or duplicated, or posted to a publicly accessible website, in whole or in part.

EXERCISE 20-12, Concluded

c. ____

____

© 2018 Cengage. May not be scanned, copied or duplicated, or posted to a publicly accessible website, in whole or in part.

EXERCISE 20-13

© 2018 Cengage. May not be scanned, copied or duplicated, or posted to a publicly accessible website, in whole or in part.

Name ____________________

EXERCISE 20-14

a. ____________________

b.

	A	B	C	D
1			Equivalent Units	
2		Whole Units	Direct Materials	Conversion
3				
4				
5				
6				
7				
8				
9				
10				
11				
12				
13				
14				
15				
16				
17				
18				

	A	B	C
1		Costs	
2		Direct Materials	Conversion
3			
4			
5			
6			
7			
8			

c. ____________________

© 2018 Cengage. May not be scanned, copied or duplicated, or posted to a publicly accessible website, in whole or in part.

EXERCISE 20-15

a. ______________________

b.

c. ______________________

d. ______________________

____

e. ______________________

____

© 2018 Cengage. May not be scanned, copied or duplicated, or posted to a publicly accessible website, in whole or in part.

Name ____________________

EXERCISE 20-16

a. 1. through 4.

	A	B	C	D
1				
2	Cost of Production Report—________			
3				
4			Equivalent Units	
5	UNITS	Whole Units	Direct Materials	Conversion
6				
7				
8				
9				
10				
11				
12				
13				
14				
15				
16				
17				
18				
19				
20				
21				
22				
23				
24				
25				
26				
27				
28				
29				
30				

© 2018 Cengage. May not be scanned, copied or duplicated, or posted to a publicly accessible website, in whole or in part.

EXERCISE 20-16, Continued

	A	B	C	D
1			Costs	
2	COSTS	Direct Materials	Conversion	Total
3				
4				
5				
6				
7				
8				
9				
10				
11				
12				
13				
14				
15				
16				
17				
18				
19				
20				
21				
22				
23				
24				
25				
26				
27				
28				
29				
30				
31				
32				
33				
34				
35				
36				
37				
38				
39				
40				

© 2018 Cengage. May not be scanned, copied or duplicated, or posted to a publicly accessible website, in whole or in part.

EXERCISE 20-16, Concluded

b.

© 2018 Cengage. May not be scanned, copied or duplicated, or posted to a publicly accessible website, in whole or in part.

EXERCISE 20-17

a.

	A	B	C	D
1				
2	**Cost of Production Report—________________**			
3				
4			**Equivalent Units**	
5	**UNITS**	**Whole Units**	**Direct Materials**	**Conversion**
6				
7				
8				
9				
10				
11				
12				
13				
14				
15				
16				
17				
18				
19				
20				
21				
22				
23				
24				
25				
26				
27				
28				
29				
30				

© 2018 Cengage. May not be scanned, copied or duplicated, or posted to a publicly accessible website, in whole or in part.

EXERCISE 20-17, Continued

	A	B	C	D
1			Costs	
2	COSTS	Direct Materials	Conversion	Total
3				
4				
5				
6				
7				
8				
9				
10				
11				
12				
13				
14				
15				
16				
17				
18				
19				
20				
21				
22				
23				
24				
25				
26				
27				
28				
29				
30				
31				
32				
33				
34				
35				
36				
37				
38				
39				
40				

© 2018 Cengage. May not be scanned, copied or duplicated, or posted to a publicly accessible website, in whole or in part.

EXERCISE 20-17, Concluded

b.

EXERCISE 20-18

a. 1. through 3.

JOURNAL PAGE

	DATE		DESCRIPTION	POST. REF.	DEBIT	CREDIT	
1							1
2							2
3							3
4							4
5							5
6							6
7							7
8							8
9							9
10							10
11							11
12							12
13							13
14							14
15							15
16							16
17							17
18							18

© 2018 Cengage. May not be scanned, copied or duplicated, or posted to a publicly accessible website, in whole or in part.

EXERCISE 20-18, Continued

Supporting calculations:

	A	B	C	D
1			Equivalent Units	
2		Whole Units	Direct Materials	Conversion
3				
4				
5				
6				
7				
8				
9				
10				
11				
12				
13				
14				
15				
16				
17				
18				

© 2018 Cengage. May not be scanned, copied or duplicated, or posted to a publicly accessible website, in whole or in part.

EXERCISE 20-18, Concluded

b. ______________________

____

____

c.

____

____

____

____

____

____

© 2018 Cengage. May not be scanned, copied or duplicated, or posted to a publicly accessible website, in whole or in part.

EXERCISE 20-19

a. 1. through 3.

JOURNAL

PAGE

	DATE		DESCRIPTION	POST. REF.	DEBIT	CREDIT	
1							1
2							2
3							3
4							4
5							5
6							6
7							7
8							8
9							9
10							10
11							11
12							12
13							13
14							14
15							15

© 2018 Cengage. May not be scanned, copied or duplicated, or posted to a publicly accessible website, in whole or in part.

EXERCISE 20-19, Continued

Supporting calculations:

	A	B	C	D
1			Equivalent Units	
2		Whole Units	Direct Materials	Conversion
3				
4				
5				
6				
7				
8				
9				
10				
11				
12				
13				
14				
15				

© 2018 Cengage. May not be scanned, copied or duplicated, or posted to a publicly accessible website, in whole or in part.

EXERCISE 20-19, Concluded

b. ______________________

____

____

© 2018 Cengage. May not be scanned, copied or duplicated, or posted to a publicly accessible website, in whole or in part.

EXERCISE 20-20

a. Cost per megawatt hour (MWh) for the fossil fuel plant:

Cost per megawatt hour (MWh) for the wind farm:

Lowest cost facility:

© 2018 Cengage. May not be scanned, copied or duplicated, or posted to a publicly accessible website, in whole or in part.

EXERCISE 20-20, Concluded

b. ______________________

c. ______________________

© 2018 Cengage. May not be scanned, copied or duplicated, or posted to a publicly accessible website, in whole or in part.

EXERCISE 20-21

	A	B	C	D	E
1					
2					
3					
4					
5					

	A	B	C	D	E
1					
2					
3					
4					
5					
6					
7					
8					
9					
10					
11					
12					

© 2018 Cengage. May not be scanned, copied or duplicated, or posted to a publicly accessible website, in whole or in part.

EXERCISE 20-21, Concluded

© 2018 Cengage. May not be scanned, copied or duplicated, or posted to a publicly accessible website, in whole or in part.

EXERCISE 20-22

a.

	A	B	C	D	E	F	G
1		**January**	**February**	**March**	**April**	**May**	**June**
2							
3							
4							
5							

© 2018 Cengage. May not be scanned, copied or duplicated, or posted to a publicly accessible website, in whole or in part.

EXERCISE 20-22, Concluded

b.

© 2018 Cengage. May not be scanned, copied or duplicated, or posted to a publicly accessible website, in whole or in part.

EXERCISE 20-23

© 2018 Cengage. May not be scanned, copied or duplicated, or posted to a publicly accessible website, in whole or in part.

EXERCISE 20-23, Concluded

APPENDIX EXERCISE 20-24

a. and b.

	A	B	C
1		a. Whole Units	b. Equivalent Units of Production
2			
3			
4			
5			
6			
7			
8			
9			
10			
11			
12			
13			
14			
15			
16			
17			
18			

© 2018 Cengage. May not be scanned, copied or duplicated, or posted to a publicly accessible website, in whole or in part.

APPENDIX EXERCISE 20-25

a. Drawing Department

	A	B	C
1		**Whole Units**	**Equivalent Units of Production**
2			
3			
4			
5			
6			
7			
8			
9			
10			
11			
12			
13			
14			
15			
16			
17			
18			

b. Winding Department

	A	B	C
1		**Whole Units**	**Equivalent Units of Production**
2			
3			
4			
5			
6			
7			
8			
9			
10			
11			
12			
13			
14			
15			
16			
17			
18			

© 2018 Cengage. May not be scanned, copied or duplicated, or posted to a publicly accessible website, in whole or in part.

APPENDIX EXERCISE 20-26

a.

b.

	A	B	C
1		**Whole Units**	**Equivalent Units of Production**
2			
3			
4			
5			
6			
7			
8			
9			
10			
11			
12			
13			
14			
15			
16			
17			
18			

© 2018 Cengage. May not be scanned, copied or duplicated, or posted to a publicly accessible website, in whole or in part.

APPENDIX EXERCISE 20-27

a. and b.

	A	B	C
1		Whole Units	Equivalent Units of Production
2			
3			
4			
5			
6			
7			
8			
9			
10			
11			
12			
13			
14			
15			
16			
17			
18			

c. ______________________________

d. ______________________________

e. ______________________________

© 2018 Cengage. May not be scanned, copied or duplicated, or posted to a publicly accessible website, in whole or in part.

APPENDIX EXERCISE 20-28

a.

	A	B	C
1		Whole Units	Equivalent Units of Production
2			
3			
4			
5			
6			
7			
8			
9			
10			
11			
12			
13			
14			
15			
16			
17			
18			

b.

c.

© 2018 Cengage. May not be scanned, copied or duplicated, or posted to a publicly accessible website, in whole or in part.

APPENDIX EXERCISE 20-29

	A	B	C
1			
2	**Cost of Production Report—________**		
3			
4	**UNITS**	**Whole Units**	**Equivalent Units of Production**
5			
6			
7			
8			
9			
10			
11			
12			
13			
14			
15			
16			
17			
18			
19			
20			
21			
22			

	A	B
1	**COSTS**	**Costs**
2		
3		
4		
5		
6		
7		
8		
9		
10		
11		
12		
13		
14		
15		
16		
17		
18		
19		
20		
21		

© 2018 Cengage. May not be scanned, copied or duplicated, or posted to a publicly accessible website, in whole or in part.

Name ______________________________

APPENDIX EXERCISE 20-30

	A	B	C
1			
2	Cost of Production Report—______________		
3			
4	UNITS	Whole Units	Equivalent Units of Production
5			
6			
7			
8			
9			
10			
11			
12			
13			
14			
15			
16			
17			
18			
19			
20			
21			
22			

	A	B
1	COSTS	Costs
2		
3		
4		
5		
6		
7		
8		
9		
10		
11		
12		
13		
14		
15		
16		
17		
18		
19		
20		
21		

© 2018 Cengage. May not be scanned, copied or duplicated, or posted to a publicly accessible website, in whole or in part.

This Page Not Used.

© 2018 Cengage. May not be scanned, copied or duplicated, or posted to a publicly accessible website, in whole or in part.

PROBLEM 20-1 ___

1. a. through i.

JOURNAL

PAGE

DATE		DESCRIPTION	POST. REF.	DEBIT	CREDIT

© 2018 Cengage. May not be scanned, copied or duplicated, or posted to a publicly accessible website, in whole or in part.

PROBLEM 20-1 ___, Continued

JOURNAL

PAGE

DATE		DESCRIPTION	POST. REF.	DEBIT	CREDIT

© 2018 Cengage. May not be scanned, copied or duplicated, or posted to a publicly accessible website, in whole or in part.

PROBLEM 20-1 ___, Concluded

2.

	MATERIALS	WORK IN PROCESS— _______ DEPT.	WORK IN PROCESS— _______ DEPT.	FINISHED GOODS

3.

	FACTORY OVERHEAD— _________ DEPT.	FACTORY OVERHEAD— _________ DEPT.

© 2018 Cengage. May not be scanned, copied or duplicated, or posted to a publicly accessible website, in whole or in part.

This Page Not Used.

© 2018 Cengage. May not be scanned, copied or duplicated, or posted to a publicly accessible website, in whole or in part.

PROBLEM 20-2 ___

1.

	A	B	C	D
1				
2	Cost of Production Report—______________			
3				
4			Equivalent Units	
5	UNITS	Whole Units	Direct Materials	Conversion
6				
7				
8				
9				
10				
11				
12				
13				
14				
15				
16				
17				
18				
19				
20				
21				
22				
23				
24				
25				
26				
27				
28				
29				
30				
31				
32				

© 2018 Cengage. May not be scanned, copied or duplicated, or posted to a publicly accessible website, in whole or in part.

PROBLEM 20-2 ___, Continued

	A	B	C	D
1			Costs	
2	COSTS	Direct Materials	Conversion	Total
3				
4				
5				
6				
7				
8				
9				
10				
11				
12				
13				
14				
15				
16				
17				
18				
19				
20				
21				
22				
23				
24				
25				
26				
27				
28				
29				
30				
31				
32				
33				
34				
35				
36				
37				
38				
39				
40				
41				
42				

© 2018 Cengage. May not be scanned, copied or duplicated, or posted to a publicly accessible website, in whole or in part.

PROBLEM 20-2 ___, Concluded

2. ______________________________

Computations:

© 2018 Cengage. May not be scanned, copied or duplicated, or posted to a publicly accessible website, in whole or in part.

This Page Not Used.

© 2018 Cengage. May not be scanned, copied or duplicated, or posted to a publicly accessible website, in whole or in part.

PROBLEM 20-3 ___

1.

	A	B	C	D
1				
2	**Cost of Production Report—______________**			
3				
4			**Equivalent Units**	
5	UNITS	**Whole Units**	**Direct Materials**	**Conversion**
6				
7				
8				
9				
10				
11				
12				
13				
14				
15				
16				
17				
18				
19				
20				
21				
22				
23				
24				
25				
26				
27				
28				
29				
30				
31				
32				

© 2018 Cengage. May not be scanned, copied or duplicated, or posted to a publicly accessible website, in whole or in part.

PROBLEM 20-3 ___, Continued

	A	B	C	D
1			Costs	
2	COSTS	Direct Materials	Conversion	Total
3				
4				
5				
6				
7				
8				
9				
10				
11				
12				
13				
14				
15				
16				
17				
18				
19				
20				
21				
22				
23				
24				
25				
26				
27				
28				
29				
30				
31				
32				
33				
34				
35				
36				
37				
38				
39				
40				
41				
42				

© 2018 Cengage. May not be scanned, copied or duplicated, or posted to a publicly accessible website, in whole or in part.

PROBLEM 20-3 ___, Concluded

2.

JOURNAL PAGE

	DATE		DESCRIPTION	POST. REF.	DEBIT	CREDIT	
1							1
2							2
3							3
4							4
5							5
6							6
7							7
8							8
9							9
10							10

3. ______________________________

4. ______________________________

© 2018 Cengage. May not be scanned, copied or duplicated, or posted to a publicly accessible website, in whole or in part.

This Page Not Used.

© 2018 Cengage. May not be scanned, copied or duplicated, or posted to a publicly accessible website, in whole or in part.

PROBLEM 20-4 ___

1. and 2.

ACCOUNT *Work in Process—____________ Department* ACCOUNT NO.

DATE		ITEM	DEBIT	CREDIT	BALANCE	
					DEBIT	CREDIT

© 2018 Cengage. May not be scanned, copied or duplicated, or posted to a publicly accessible website, in whole or in part.

PROBLEM 20-4 ___, Continued

1.

	A	B	C	D
1				
2	Cost of Production Report—________________			
3				
4			Equivalent Units	
5	UNITS	Whole Units	Direct Materials (a)	Conversion (a)
6				
7				
8				
9				
10				
11				
12				
13				
14				
15				
16				
17				
18				
19				
20				
21				
22				
23				
24				
25				
26				
27				
28				
29				
30				
31				
32				

© 2018 Cengage. May not be scanned, copied or duplicated, or posted to a publicly accessible website, in whole or in part.

PROBLEM 20-4 ___, Continued

	A	B	C	D
1		Costs		
2	COSTS	Direct Materials	Conversion	Total
3				
4				
5				
6				
7				
8				
9				
10				
11				
12				
13				
14				
15				
16				
17				
18				
19				
20				
21				
22				
23				
24				
25				
26				
27				
28				
29				
30				
31				
32				
33				
34				
35				
36				
37				
38				
39				
40				
41				
42				

© 2018 Cengage. May not be scanned, copied or duplicated, or posted to a publicly accessible website, in whole or in part.

PROBLEM 20-4 ___, Continued

2.

	A	B	C	D
1				
2	**Cost of Production Report—________________**			
3				
4			**Equivalent Units**	
5	**UNITS**	**Whole Units**	**Direct Materials (a)**	**Conversion (a)**
6				
7				
8				
9				
10				
11				
12				
13				
14				
15				
16				
17				
18				
19				
20				
21				
22				
23				
24				
25				
26				
27				
28				
29				
30				
31				
32				

© 2018 Cengage. May not be scanned, copied or duplicated, or posted to a publicly accessible website, in whole or in part.

PROBLEM 20-4 ___, Continued

	A	B	C	D
1			Costs	
2	COSTS	Direct Materials	Conversion	Total
3				
4				
5				
6				
7				
8				
9				
10				
11				
12				
13				
14				
15				
16				
17				
18				
19				
20				
21				
22				
23				
24				
25				
26				
27				
28				
29				
30				
31				
32				
33				
34				
35				
36				
37				
38				
39				
40				
41				
42				

© 2018 Cengage. May not be scanned, copied or duplicated, or posted to a publicly accessible website, in whole or in part.

PROBLEM 20-4 ___, Concluded

3. ____

© 2018 Cengage. May not be scanned, copied or duplicated, or posted to a publicly accessible website, in whole or in part.

APPENDIX PROBLEM 20-5 ___

	A	B	C
1			
2	Cost of Production Report—_______________		
3			
4	UNITS	Whole Units	Equivalent Units of Production
5			
6			
7			
8			
9			
10			
11			
12			
13			
14			
15			
16			
17			
18			
19			
20			
21			
22			

	A	B
1	COSTS	Costs
2		
3		
4		
5		
6		
7		
8		
9		
10		
11		
12		
13		
14		
15		
16		
17		
18		
19		
20		
21		

© 2018 Cengage. May not be scanned, copied or duplicated, or posted to a publicly accessible website, in whole or in part.

This Page Not Used.

© 2018 Cengage. May not be scanned, copied or duplicated, or posted to a publicly accessible website, in whole or in part.

EXERCISE 21-1

1. ____________________
2. ____________________
3. ____________________
4. ____________________
5. ____________________
6. ____________________
7. ____________________
8. ____________________
9. ____________________
10. ____________________
11. ____________________
12. ____________________
13. ____________________
14. ____________________
15. ____________________

EXERCISE 21-2

a. ____________________
b. ____________________
c. ____________________
d. ____________________
e. ____________________

EXERCISE 21-3

1. Instructor salaries: ____________________
2. Admissions office salaries: ____________________
3. Student records office salaries: ____________________
4. Financial aid office salaries: ____________________
5. Housing personnel wages: ____________________
6. Office supplies: ____________________

EXERCISE 21-4

1. Preparation costs for each car received: ____________________
2. Salespersons' commission of 5% of the sales price for each car sold: ____________________
3. Administrative costs for ordering cars: ____________________

EXERCISE 21-5

a. ____________________
b. ____________________
c. ____________________
d. ____________________
e. ____________________
f. ____________________
g. ____________________
h. ____________________
i. ____________________
j. ____________________

© 2018 Cengage. May not be scanned, copied or duplicated, or posted to a publicly accessible website, in whole or in part.

EXERCISE 21-6

	45,000	60,000	75,000
Components produced	45,000	60,000	75,000
Total costs:			
Total variable costs	$1,350,000	(d) ____________	(j) ____________
Total fixed costs	810,000	(e) ____________	(k) ____________
Total costs	$2,160,000	(f) ____________	(l) ____________
Cost per unit:			
Variable cost per unit	(a) ____________	(g) ____________	(m) ____________
Fixed cost per unit	(b) ____________	(h) ____________	(n) ____________
Total cost per unit	(c) ____________	(i) ____________	(o) ____________

Supporting calculations:

© 2018 Cengage. May not be scanned, copied or duplicated, or posted to a publicly accessible website, in whole or in part.

Name ______________________________

EXERCISE 21-7

a. Variable Cost per Unit: ______________________________

Fixed Cost: ______________________________

b. ______________________________

© 2018 Cengage. May not be scanned, copied or duplicated, or posted to a publicly accessible website, in whole or in part.

EXERCISE 21-8

Variable Cost per Gross-Ton Mile: ______________________________

Fixed Cost: ______________________________

© 2018 Cengage. May not be scanned, copied or duplicated, or posted to a publicly accessible website, in whole or in part.

EXERCISE 21-9

a.

____

____

____

____

____

b.

EXERCISE 21-10

a.

b. ______________________________

____

____

____

____

© 2018 Cengage. May not be scanned, copied or duplicated, or posted to a publicly accessible website, in whole or in part.

EXERCISE 21-10, Concluded

c.

EXERCISE 21-11

a. ______________________________

____

____

____

____

b. ______________________________

____

____

____

____

____

____

© 2018 Cengage. May not be scanned, copied or duplicated, or posted to a publicly accessible website, in whole or in part.

EXERCISE 21-12

a. ____

© 2018 Cengage. May not be scanned, copied or duplicated, or posted to a publicly accessible website, in whole or in part.

EXERCISE 21-12, Concluded

b. ____

____

____

____

____

Calculations:

© 2018 Cengage. May not be scanned, copied or duplicated, or posted to a publicly accessible website, in whole or in part.

EXERCISE 21-13

a. ______________________________

b. ______________________________

EXERCISE 21-14

© 2018 Cengage. May not be scanned, copied or duplicated, or posted to a publicly accessible website, in whole or in part.

EXERCISE 21-15

© 2018 Cengage. May not be scanned, copied or duplicated, or posted to a publicly accessible website, in whole or in part.

Name ____________________

EXERCISE 21-16

a. ____________________

Calculations:

© 2018 Cengage. May not be scanned, copied or duplicated, or posted to a publicly accessible website, in whole or in part.

EXERCISE 21-16, Concluded

b.

© 2018 Cengage. May not be scanned, copied or duplicated, or posted to a publicly accessible website, in whole or in part.

EXERCISE 21-17

a.

Sales and Costs

Units of Sales

b. ______________________________

____

c. ______________________________

____

____

____

© 2018 Cengage. May not be scanned, copied or duplicated, or posted to a publicly accessible website, in whole or in part.

EXERCISE 21-18

a. ____

____

b.

c.

Operating Profit (Loss)

Units of Sales

d. ____

____

© 2018 Cengage. May not be scanned, copied or duplicated, or posted to a publicly accessible website, in whole or in part.

EXERCISE 21-19

Chart name: ______________________

a. ______________________

b. ______________________

c. ______________________

d. ______________________

e. ______________________

f. ______________________

EXERCISE 21-20

Chart name: ______________________

a. ______________________

b. ______________________

c. ______________________

d. ______________________

e. ______________________

f. ______________________

EXERCISE 21-21

a. ______________________

b. Baseball bats: ______________________

Baseball gloves: ______________________

© 2018 Cengage. May not be scanned, copied or duplicated, or posted to a publicly accessible website, in whole or in part.

EXERCISE 21-22

a.

Supporting calculations:

b.

© 2018 Cengage. May not be scanned, copied or duplicated, or posted to a publicly accessible website, in whole or in part.

EXERCISE 21-23

a. (1) In dollars: ______________________

(2) As a percentage of sales: ______________________

b. ______________________

EXERCISE 21-24

© 2018 Cengage. May not be scanned, copied or duplicated, or posted to a publicly accessible website, in whole or in part.

EXERCISE 21-25

a. Beck Inc.: ______________________________

Bryant Inc.: ______________________________

b. ______________________________

c. ______________________________

APPENDIX EXERCISE 21-26

a. ______________________________

b. ______________________________

c. ______________________________

© 2018 Cengage. May not be scanned, copied or duplicated, or posted to a publicly accessible website, in whole or in part.

APPENDIX EXERCISE 21-27

a.

Income Statement—Variable Costing

Computations:

© 2018 Cengage. May not be scanned, copied or duplicated, or posted to a publicly accessible website, in whole or in part.

APPENDIX EXERCISE 21-27, Concluded

b.

© 2018 Cengage. May not be scanned, copied or duplicated, or posted to a publicly accessible website, in whole or in part.

APPENDIX EXERCISE 21-28

a.

Income Statement—Absorption Costing

Computations:

© 2018 Cengage. May not be scanned, copied or duplicated, or posted to a publicly accessible website, in whole or in part.

APPENDIX EXERCISE 21-28, Concluded

b.

© 2018 Cengage. May not be scanned, copied or duplicated, or posted to a publicly accessible website, in whole or in part.

PROBLEM 21-1 ___

Cost	Fixed Cost	Variable Cost	Mixed Cost
a.			
b.			
c.			
d.			
e.			
f.			
g.			
h.			
i.			
j.			
k.			
l.			
m.			
n.			
o.			
p.			
q.			
r.			
s.			
t.			

© 2018 Cengage. May not be scanned, copied or duplicated, or posted to a publicly accessible website, in whole or in part.

This Page Not Used.

© 2018 Cengage. May not be scanned, copied or duplicated, or posted to a publicly accessible website, in whole or in part.

PROBLEM 21-2 ___

1.

2.

a. Unit variable cost: ______________________

b. Unit contribution margin: ______________________

3. ______________________

© 2018 Cengage. May not be scanned, copied or duplicated, or posted to a publicly accessible website, in whole or in part.

PROBLEM 21-2 ___, Continued

4.

5.

6.

7.

© 2018 Cengage. May not be scanned, copied or duplicated, or posted to a publicly accessible website, in whole or in part.

PROBLEM 21-2 ___, Concluded

8. ____

© 2018 Cengage. May not be scanned, copied or duplicated, or posted to a publicly accessible website, in whole or in part.

This Page Not Used.

© 2018 Cengage. May not be scanned, copied or duplicated, or posted to a publicly accessible website, in whole or in part.

PROBLEM 21-3 ___

1. ______________________

2. ______________________

© 2018 Cengage. May not be scanned, copied or duplicated, or posted to a publicly accessible website, in whole or in part.

PROBLEM 21-3 ___, Concluded

3.

Sales and Costs

Units of Sales

4.

© 2018 Cengage. May not be scanned, copied or duplicated, or posted to a publicly accessible website, in whole or in part.

PROBLEM 21-4 ___

1.

Sales and Costs

Units of Sales

© 2018 Cengage. May not be scanned, copied or duplicated, or posted to a publicly accessible website, in whole or in part.

PROBLEM 21-4 ___, Continued

© 2018 Cengage. May not be scanned, copied or duplicated, or posted to a publicly accessible website, in whole or in part.

PROBLEM 21-4 ___, Continued

2.

Sales and Costs

Units of Sales

© 2018 Cengage. May not be scanned, copied or duplicated, or posted to a publicly accessible website, in whole or in part.

PROBLEM 21-4 ___, Continued

3.

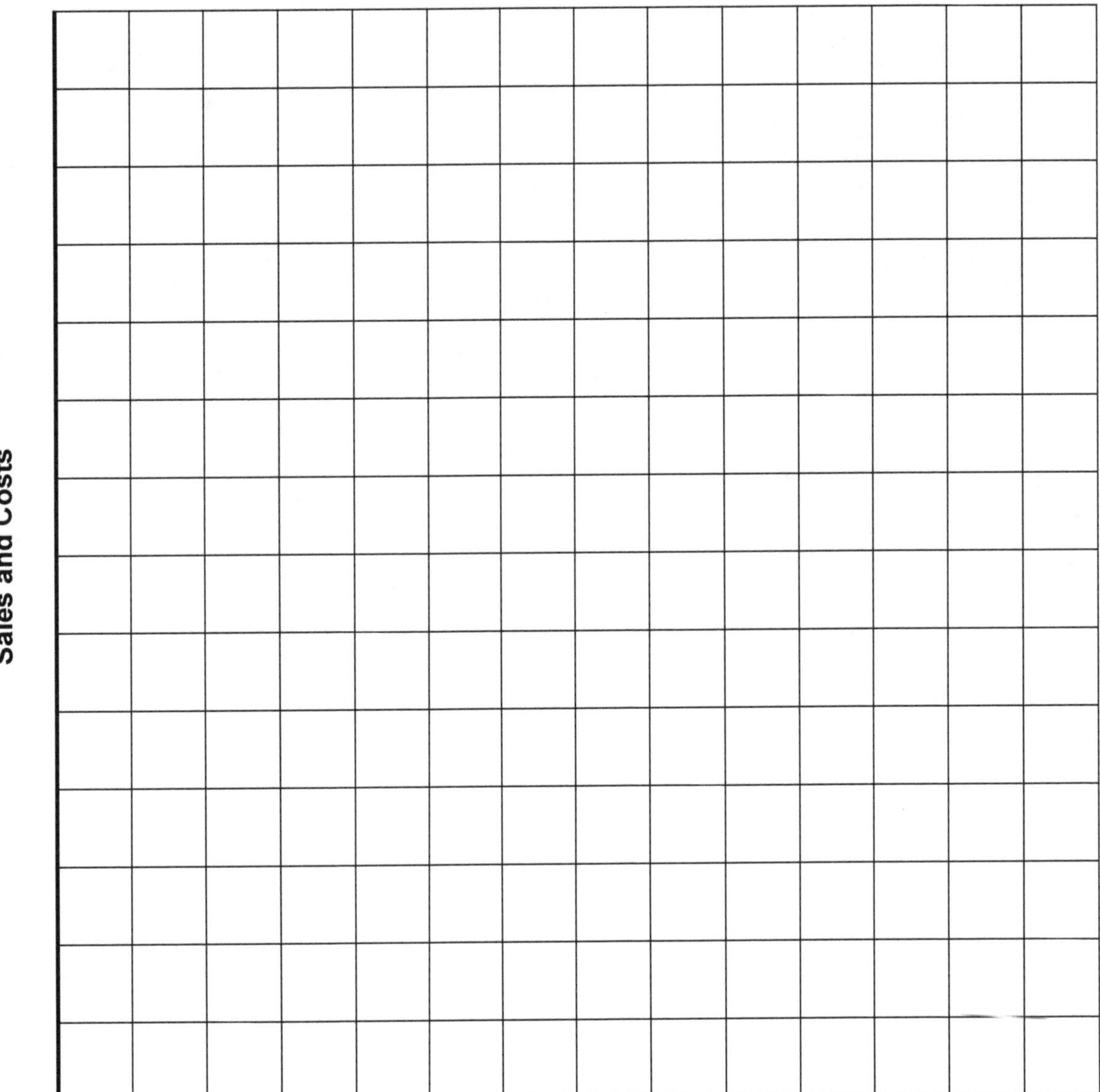

© 2018 Cengage. May not be scanned, copied or duplicated, or posted to a publicly accessible website, in whole or in part.

PROBLEM 21-4 ___, Continued

© 2018 Cengage. May not be scanned, copied or duplicated, or posted to a publicly accessible website, in whole or in part.

PROBLEM 21-4 ___, Concluded

4.

Sales and Costs

Units of Sales

© 2018 Cengage. May not be scanned, copied or duplicated, or posted to a publicly accessible website, in whole or in part.

PROBLEM 21-5 ___

1.

2.

© 2018 Cengage. May not be scanned, copied or duplicated, or posted to a publicly accessible website, in whole or in part.

PROBLEM 21-5 ___, Concluded

3.

© 2018 Cengage. May not be scanned, copied or duplicated, or posted to a publicly accessible website, in whole or in part.

PROBLEM 21-6 ___

1.

Estimated Income Statement

© 2018 Cengage. May not be scanned, copied or duplicated, or posted to a publicly accessible website, in whole or in part.

PROBLEM 21-6 ___, Continued

2. ______________________________

3. ______________________________

© 2018 Cengage. May not be scanned, copied or duplicated, or posted to a publicly accessible website, in whole or in part.

PROBLEM 21-6 ___, Continued

4.

Sales and Costs

Units

© 2018 Cengage. May not be scanned, copied or duplicated, or posted to a publicly accessible website, in whole or in part.

PROBLEM 21-6 ___, Concluded

5.

6.

© 2018 Cengage. May not be scanned, copied or duplicated, or posted to a publicly accessible website, in whole or in part.

EXERCISE 22-1

a.

	A	B	C	D	E
1	**KATHERINE MALLOY**				
2	**Cash Budget**				
3	**For the Four Months Ending December 31**				
4		**September**	**October**	**November**	**December**
5					
6					
7					
8					
9					
10					
11					
12					
13					
14					
15					
16					
17					
18					
19					
20					
21					
22					
23					
24					
25					
26					
27					
28					

b. ____

____

____

© 2018 Cengage. May not be scanned, copied or duplicated, or posted to a publicly accessible website, in whole or in part.

EXERCISE 22-1, Concluded

c.

© 2018 Cengage. May not be scanned, copied or duplicated, or posted to a publicly accessible website, in whole or in part.

EXERCISE 22-2

	A	B	C	D
1	**MORNINGSIDE TECHNOLOGIES INC.**			
2	**Flexible Selling and Administrative Expenses Budget**			
3	**For the Month Ending April 30**			
4				
5				
6				
7				
8				
9				
10				
11				
12				
13				
14				
15				
16				
17				
18				
19				
20				
21				
22				
23				
24				
25				
26				
27				
28				

© 2018 Cengage. May not be scanned, copied or duplicated, or posted to a publicly accessible website, in whole or in part.

EXERCISE 22-3

a.

	A	B	C	D
1	NILAND COMPANY—MACHINING DEPARTMENT			
2	Flexible Production Budget			
3	For the Three Months Ending March 31			
4		January	February	March
5				
6				
7				
8				
9				
10				
11				
12				
13				
14				
15				
16				
17				
18				
19				
20				
21				
22				
23				
24				
25				

© 2018 Cengage. May not be scanned, copied or duplicated, or posted to a publicly accessible website, in whole or in part.

EXERCISE 22-3, Concluded

b.

	JANUARY	FEBRUARY	MARCH

EXERCISE 22-4

	A	B	C	D
1	STEELCASE INC.—ASSEMBLY DEPARTMENT			
2	Flexible Production Budget			
3	For the Month Ending August 31			
4	(assumed data)			
5				
6				
7				
8				
9				
10				
11				
12				
13				
14				
15				
16				
17				
18				

© 2018 Cengage. May not be scanned, copied or duplicated, or posted to a publicly accessible website, in whole or in part.

EXERCISE 22-5

	A	B	C
1	WEIGHTLESS INC.		
2	Production Budget		
3	For the Month Ending October 31		
4		Units	
5		Bath Scale	Gym Scale
6			
7			
8			
9			
10			
11			
12			
13			

EXERCISE 22-6

a.

	A	B	C	D
1	SONIC INC.			
2	Sales Budget			
3	For the Month Ending June 30			
4	Product and Area	Unit Sales Volume	Unit Selling Price	Total Sales
5				
6				
7				
8				
9				
10				
11				
12				
13				
14				

© 2018 Cengage. May not be scanned, copied or duplicated, or posted to a publicly accessible website, in whole or in part.

EXERCISE 22-6, Concluded

b.

	A	B	C
1	SONIC INC.		
2	Production Budget		
3	For the Month Ending June 30		
4		Units	
5		Model Rumble	Model Thunder
6			
7			
8			
9			
10			
11			
12			
13			

EXERCISE 22-7

	A	B	C	D
1	ROLLINS AND COHEN, CPAs			
2	Professional Fees Earned Budget			
3	For the Year Ending December 31, 20Y7			
4		Billable Hours	Hourly Rate	Total Revenue
5				
6				
7				
8				
9				
10				
11				
12				
13				
14				
15				
16				
17				
18				
19				
20				
21				
22				

© 2018 Cengage. May not be scanned, copied or duplicated, or posted to a publicly accessible website, in whole or in part.

EXERCISE 22-8

	A	B	C
1	ROLLINS AND COHEN, CPAs		
2	Professional Labor Cost Budget		
3	For the Year Ending December 31, 20Y7		
4		Staff	Partners
5			
6			
7			
8			
9			
10			
11			
12			
13			

EXERCISE 22-9

	A	B	C	D	E
1	LORENZO'S FROZEN PIZZA INC.				
2	Direct Materials Purchases Budget				
3	For the Month Ending September 30				
4		Dough	Tomato	Cheese	Total
5					
6					
7					
8					
9					
10					
11					
12					
13					
14					
15					
16					
17					
18					
19					
20					
21					
22					
23					
24					
25					
26					
27					
28					

© 2018 Cengage. May not be scanned, copied or duplicated, or posted to a publicly accessible website, in whole or in part.

Name ________________________________

EXERCISE 22-10

	A	B	C	D
1	**COCA-COLA ENTERPRISES—WAKEFIELD PLANT**			
2	**Direct Materials Purchases Budget**			
3	**For the Month Ending May 31**			
4	**(assumed data)**			
5		**Concentrate**	**2-Liter Bottles**	**Carbonated Water**
6				
7				
8				
9				
10				
11				
12				
13				
14				
15				

Supporting calculations:

© 2018 Cengage. May not be scanned, copied or duplicated, or posted to a publicly accessible website, in whole or in part.

EXERCISE 22-11

	A	B	C	D
1	SAFETY GRIP COMPANY			
2	Direct Materials Purchases Budget			
3	For the Year Ending December 31, 20Y8			
4		Rubber	Steel Belts	Total
5				
6				
7				
8				
9				
10				
11				
12				
13				
14				
15				
16				
17				
18				
19				
20				
21				
22				
23				
24				
25				
26				
27				
28				

© 2018 Cengage. May not be scanned, copied or duplicated, or posted to a publicly accessible website, in whole or in part.

EXERCISE 22-12

	A	B	C
1	MATCHPOINT RACKET COMPANY		
2	Direct Labor Cost Budget		
3	For the Month Ending March 31		
4		Forming Department	Assembly Department
5			
6			
7			
8			
9			
10			
11			
12			
13			
14			
15			
16			
17			
18			
19			
20			

© 2018 Cengage. May not be scanned, copied or duplicated, or posted to a publicly accessible website, in whole or in part.

EXERCISE 22-13

	A	B	C
1	**AMBASSADOR SUITES INC.**		
2	**Direct Labor Cost Budget**		
3	**For a Weekday or a Weekend Day**		
4		**Weekday**	**Weekend Day**
5			
6			
7			
8			
9			
10			
11			
12			
13			
14			
15			
16			
17			
18			
19			
20			
21			
22			
23			
24			
25			
26			
27			
28			
29			
30			

© 2018 Cengage. May not be scanned, copied or duplicated, or posted to a publicly accessible website, in whole or in part.

EXERCISE 22-14

a.

	A	B	C
1	LEVI STRAUSS & CO.		
2	Production Budget		
3	For the Month Ending May 31		
4	(assumed data)		
5		Dockers®	501® Jeans
6			
7			
8			
9			
10			
11			
12			
13			
14			
15			

© 2018 Cengage. May not be scanned, copied or duplicated, or posted to a publicly accessible website, in whole or in part.

EXERCISE 22-14, Concluded

b.

	A	B	C	D	E	F
1	LEVI STRAUSS & CO.					
2	Direct Labor Cost Budget					
3	For the Month Ending May 31					
4	(assumed data)					
5		Inseam	Outerseam	Pockets	Zipper	Total
6						
7						
8						
9						
10						
11						
12						
13						
14						
15						
16						
17						
18						
19						
20						
21						
22						
23						
24						
25						
26						
27						
28						
29						
30						
31						
32						
33						
34						
35						

© 2018 Cengage. May not be scanned, copied or duplicated, or posted to a publicly accessible website, in whole or in part.

EXERCISE 22-15

	A	B	C
1	SWEET TOOTH CANDY COMPANY		
2	Factory Overhead Cost Budget		
3	For the Month Ending August 31		
4			
5			
6			
7			
8			
9			
10			
11			
12			
13			
14			
15			
16			
17			
18			
19			
20			
21			
22			
23			
24			

© 2018 Cengage. May not be scanned, copied or duplicated, or posted to a publicly accessible website, in whole or in part.

EXERCISE 22-16

	A	B	C	D
1	**WILMINGTON CHEMICAL COMPANY**			
2	**Cost of Goods Sold Budget**			
3	**For the Month Ending June 30**			
4				
5				
6				
7				
8				
9				
10				
11				
12				
13				
14				
15				
16				
17				
18				
19				
20				
21				
22				
23				
24				
25				
26				
27				
28				
29				
30				
31				
32				
33				
34				
35				
36				

© 2018 Cengage. May not be scanned, copied or duplicated, or posted to a publicly accessible website, in whole or in part.

EXERCISE 22-17

	A	B	C	D
1	MINGWARE CERAMICS INC.			
2	Cost of Goods Sold Budget			
3	For the Month Ending September 30			
4				
5				
6				
7				
8				
9				
10				
11				
12				
13				
14				
15				
16				
17				
18				
19				
20				
21				
22				
23				
24				
25				
26				
27				
28				
29				
30				
31				
32				
33				
34				

© 2018 Cengage. May not be scanned, copied or duplicated, or posted to a publicly accessible website, in whole or in part.

EXERCISE 22-18

	A	B	C	D
1	FURRY FRIENDS SUPPLIES INC.			
2	Schedule of Collections from Sales			
3	For the Three Months Ending July 31			
4		May	June	July
5				
6				
7				
8				
9				
10				
11				
12				
13				
14				
15				
16				
17				
18				
19				
20				
21				
22				
23				
24				

© 2018 Cengage. May not be scanned, copied or duplicated, or posted to a publicly accessible website, in whole or in part.

EXERCISE 22-19

	A	B	C	D
1	OFFICE WORLD INC.			
2	Schedule of Collections from Sales			
3	For the Three Months Ending December 31			
4		October	November	December
5				
6				
7				
8				
9				
10				
11				
12				
13				
14				
15				
16				
17				
18				
19				
20				
21				
22				
23				
24				
25				
26				
27				
28				
29				
30				
31				
32				

© 2018 Cengage. May not be scanned, copied or duplicated, or posted to a publicly accessible website, in whole or in part.

EXERCISE 22-20

	A	B	C	D
1	SAFEMARK FINANCIAL INC.			
2	Schedule of Cash Payments for Selling and Administrative Expenses			
3	For the Three Months Ending May 31			
4		March	April	May
5				
6				
7				
8				
9				
10				
11				
12				
13				
14				
15				
16				
17				
18				
19				
20				
21				
22				
23				
24				

© 2018 Cengage. May not be scanned, copied or duplicated, or posted to a publicly accessible website, in whole or in part.

EXERCISE 22-21

	A	B	C	D
1	EASTGATE PHYSICAL THERAPY INC.			
2	Schedule of Cash Payments for Operations			
3	For the Three Months Ending March 31			
4		January	February	March
5				
6				
7				
8				
9				
10				
11				
12				
13				
14				
15				
16				
17				
18				
19				
20				
21				
22				
23				
24				

EXERCISE 22-22

	A	B	C	D	E
1	OMICRON INC.				
2	Capital Expenditures Budget				
3	For the Four Years Ending December 31, 20Y2–20Y5				
4		20Y2	20Y3	20Y4	20Y5
5					
6					
7					
8					
9					
10					
11					
12					
13					

© 2018 Cengage. May not be scanned, copied or duplicated, or posted to a publicly accessible website, in whole or in part.

This Page Not Used.

© 2018 Cengage. May not be scanned, copied or duplicated, or posted to a publicly accessible website, in whole or in part.

PROBLEM 22-1 ___

1.

	UNIT SALES, YEAR ENDED 20Y___		INCREASE (DECREASE) ACTUAL OVER BUDGET	
	BUDGET	ACTUAL SALES	AMOUNT	PERCENT

2.

	20Y___ ACTUAL UNITS	PERCENTAGE INCREASE (DECREASE)	20Y___ BUDGETED UNITS (ROUNDED)

© 2018 Cengage. May not be scanned, copied or duplicated, or posted to a publicly accessible website, in whole or in part.

PROBLEM 22-1 ___, Concluded

3.

	A	B	C	D
1				
2	**Sales Budget**			
3				
4	**Product and Area**	**Unit Sales Volume**	**Unit Selling Price**	**Total Sales**
5				
6				
7				
8				
9				
10				
11				
12				
13				
14				
15				
16				
17				
18				
19				
20				

© 2018 Cengage. May not be scanned, copied or duplicated, or posted to a publicly accessible website, in whole or in part.

Name ____________________

PROBLEM 22-2 ___

1.

	A	B	C	D
1				
2	Sales Budget			
3				
4	Product and Area	Unit Sales Volume	Unit Selling Price	Total Sales
5				
6				
7				
8				
9				
10				
11				
12				
13				
14				
15				
16				
17				
18				

2.

	A	B	C
1			
2	Production Budget		
3			
4		Units	
5			
6			
7			
8			
9			
10			
11			
12			
13			
14			
15			
16			

© 2018 Cengage. May not be scanned, copied or duplicated, or posted to a publicly accessible website, in whole or in part.

PROBLEM 22-2 ___, Continued

3.

	A	B	C	D	E	F
1						
2	**Direct Materials Purchases Budget**					
3						
4						
5						
6						
7						
8						
9						
10						
11						
12						
13						
14						
15						
16						
17						
18						
19						
20						
21						
22						
23						
24						
25						
26						
27						
28						
29						
30						
31						
32						
33						
34						
35						
36						

© 2018 Cengage. May not be scanned, copied or duplicated, or posted to a publicly accessible website, in whole or in part.

PROBLEM 22-2 ___, Concluded

4.

	A	B	C	D	E
1					
2	Direct Labor Cost Budget				
3					
4		________ Department	________ Department	________ Department	Total
5					
6					
7					
8					
9					
10					
11					
12					
13					
14					
15					
16					
17					
18					
19					
20					

© 2018 Cengage. May not be scanned, copied or duplicated, or posted to a publicly accessible website, in whole or in part.

This Page Not Used.

© 2018 Cengage. May not be scanned, copied or duplicated, or posted to a publicly accessible website, in whole or in part.

PROBLEM 22-3 ___

1.

	A	B	C	D
1				
2	Sales Budget			
3				
4		Unit Sales Volume	Unit Selling Price	Total Sales
5				
6				
7				
8				

2.

	A	B	C
1			
2	Production Budget		
3			
4		Units	
5			
6			
7			
8			
9			
10			
11			
12			
13			
14			

© 2018 Cengage. May not be scanned, copied or duplicated, or posted to a publicly accessible website, in whole or in part.

PROBLEM 22-3 ___, Continued

3.

	A	B	C	D
1				
2	Direct Materials Purchases Budget			
3				
4				Total
5				
6				
7				
8				
9				
10				
11				
12				
13				
14				
15				
16				
17				
18				
19				
20				
21				
22				
23				
24				

© 2018 Cengage. May not be scanned, copied or duplicated, or posted to a publicly accessible website, in whole or in part.

PROBLEM 22-3 ___, Continued

4.

	A	B	C	D
1				
2	Direct Labor Cost Budget			
3				
4		________ Department	________ Department	Total
5				
6				
7				
8				
9				
10				
11				
12				
13				
14				
15				
16				
17				
18				
19				
20				

5.

	A	B
1		
2	Factory Overhead Cost Budget	
3		
4		
5		
6		
7		
8		
9		
10		

© 2018 Cengage. May not be scanned, copied or duplicated, or posted to a publicly accessible website, in whole or in part.

PROBLEM 22-3 ___, Continued

6.

	A	B	C	D
1				
2	Cost of Goods Sold Budget			
3				
4				
5				
6				
7				
8				
9				
10				
11				
12				
13				
14				
15				
16				
17				
18				
19				
20				
21				
22				
23				
24				
25				
26				
27				
28				
29				
30				
31				
32				
33				
34				

© 2018 Cengage. May not be scanned, copied or duplicated, or posted to a publicly accessible website, in whole or in part.

PROBLEM 22-3 ___, Continued

Supporting calculations:

7.

	A	B	C
1			
2	**Selling and Administrative Expenses Budget**		
3			
4			
5			
6			
7			
8			
9			
10			
11			
12			
13			
14			
15			
16			
17			
18			
19			
20			
21			
22			
23			
24			

© 2018 Cengage. May not be scanned, copied or duplicated, or posted to a publicly accessible website, in whole or in part.

PROBLEM 22-3 ___, Concluded

8.

	A	B	C
1			
2	**Budgeted Income Statement**		
3			
4			
5			
6			
7			
8			
9			
10			
11			
12			
13			
14			
15			
16			
17			
18			
19			
20			

© 2018 Cengage. May not be scanned, copied or duplicated, or posted to a publicly accessible website, in whole or in part.

PROBLEM 22-4 ___

1.

	A	B	C	D
1				
2	**Cash Budget**			
3				
4				
5				
6				
7				
8				
9				
10				
11				
12				
13				
14				
15				
16				
17				
18				
19				
20				
21				
22				
23				
24				
25				
26				
27				
28				
29				
30				
31				
32				

© 2018 Cengage. May not be scanned, copied or duplicated, or posted to a publicly accessible website, in whole or in part.

PROBLEM 22-4 ___, Continued

Computations:

© 2018 Cengage. May not be scanned, copied or duplicated, or posted to a publicly accessible website, in whole or in part.

PROBLEM 22-4 ___, Concluded

2. ____

© 2018 Cengage. May not be scanned, copied or duplicated, or posted to a publicly accessible website, in whole or in part.

This Page Not Used.

© 2018 Cengage. May not be scanned, copied or duplicated, or posted to a publicly accessible website, in whole or in part.

PROBLEM 22-5 ___

1.

	A	B	C	D
1				
2	**Budgeted Income Statement**			
3				
4				
5				
6				
7				
8				
9				
10				
11				
12				
13				
14				
15				
16				
17				
18				
19				
20				
21				
22				
23				
24				
25				
26				
27				
28				
29				
30				
31				
32				
33				
34				
35				
36				
37				
38				
39				
40				
41				
42				

© 2018 Cengage. May not be scanned, copied or duplicated, or posted to a publicly accessible website, in whole or in part.

PROBLEM 22-5 ___, Continued

2.

	A	B	C	D
1				
2	**Budgeted Balance Sheet**			
3				
4				
5				
6				
7				
8				
9				
10				
11				
12				
13				
14				
15				
16				
17				
18				
19				
20				
21				
22				
23				
24				
25				
26				
27				
28				

© 2018 Cengage. May not be scanned, copied or duplicated, or posted to a publicly accessible website, in whole or in part.

PROBLEM 22-5 ___, Concluded

Supporting calculations:

© 2018 Cengage. May not be scanned, copied or duplicated, or posted to a publicly accessible website, in whole or in part.

This Page Not Used.

© 2018 Cengage. May not be scanned, copied or duplicated, or posted to a publicly accessible website, in whole or in part.

Name ______________________________

EXERCISE 23-1

Ingredient	Quantity	×	Price	Total
		×		
		×		
		×		

EXERCISE 23-2

a.

b.

© 2018 Cengage. May not be scanned, copied or duplicated, or posted to a publicly accessible website, in whole or in part.

EXERCISE 23-3

a.

	A	B
1	GENIE IN A BOTTLE COMPANY	
2	Manufacturing Cost Budget	
3	For the Month Ended July 31	
4		Standard Cost at Planned Volume (400,000 Bottles)
5		
6		
7		
8		
9		
10		
11		
12		
13		
14		
15		
16		

b.

	A	B	C	D
1	GENIE IN A BOTTLE COMPANY			
2	Manufacturing Costs—Budget Performance Report			
3	For the Month Ended July 31			
4		Actual Costs	Standard Cost at Actual Volume (406,000 Bottles)	Cost Variance—(Favorable) Unfavorable
5				
6				
7				
8				
9				
10				
11				
12				
13				
14				
15				
16				
17				
18				

© 2018 Cengage. May not be scanned, copied or duplicated, or posted to a publicly accessible website, in whole or in part.

EXERCISE 23-3, Concluded

c. ____________________

EXERCISE 23-4

a. Price variance: ____________________

Quantity variance: ____________________

Total direct materials cost variance: ____________________

© 2018 Cengage. May not be scanned, copied or duplicated, or posted to a publicly accessible website, in whole or in part.

EXERCISE 23-4, Concluded

b. ______________________

© 2018 Cengage. May not be scanned, copied or duplicated, or posted to a publicly accessible website, in whole or in part.

EXERCISE 23-5

Price variance: ______________________

Quantity variance: ______________________

Total direct materials cost variance: ______________________

© 2018 Cengage. May not be scanned, copied or duplicated, or posted to a publicly accessible website, in whole or in part.

EXERCISE 23-6

Alternate solution:

Alternative Solution for Standard Price:

© 2018 Cengage. May not be scanned, copied or duplicated, or posted to a publicly accessible website, in whole or in part.

EXERCISE 23-7

a.

b.

© 2018 Cengage. May not be scanned, copied or duplicated, or posted to a publicly accessible website, in whole or in part.

EXERCISE 23-8

a. Rate variance:

Time variance:

Total direct labor cost variance:

b.

© 2018 Cengage. May not be scanned, copied or duplicated, or posted to a publicly accessible website, in whole or in part.

EXERCISE 23-9

a. Rate variance: ______________________

Time variance: ______________________

Total direct labor cost variance: ______________________

b. Debit to Work in Process: ______________________

© 2018 Cengage. May not be scanned, copied or duplicated, or posted to a publicly accessible website, in whole or in part.

EXERCISE 23-10

a. (1) Cutting Department

Rate variance: ____________________

Time variance: ____________________

Total direct labor cost variance: ____________________

© 2018 Cengage. May not be scanned, copied or duplicated, or posted to a publicly accessible website, in whole or in part.

EXERCISE 23-10, Continued

(2) Sewing Department

Rate variance: ____________________

Time variance: ____________________

Total direct labor cost variance: ____________________

© 2018 Cengage. May not be scanned, copied or duplicated, or posted to a publicly accessible website, in whole or in part.

EXERCISE 23-10, Concluded

b.

© 2018 Cengage. May not be scanned, copied or duplicated, or posted to a publicly accessible website, in whole or in part.

EXERCISE 23-11

a. ______________________________

____

b.

c.

____

____

____

____

____

© 2018 Cengage. May not be scanned, copied or duplicated, or posted to a publicly accessible website, in whole or in part.

EXERCISE 23-12

a. ______________________________

b. ______________________________

© 2018 Cengage. May not be scanned, copied or duplicated, or posted to a publicly accessible website, in whole or in part.

EXERCISE 23-13

a. Rate variance:

Time variance:

Total direct labor cost variance:

© 2018 Cengage. May not be scanned, copied or duplicated, or posted to a publicly accessible website, in whole or in part.

EXERCISE 23-13, Concluded

b. ____________________

© 2018 Cengage. May not be scanned, copied or duplicated, or posted to a publicly accessible website, in whole or in part.

EXERCISE 23-14

Step 1: ______________________________

Step 2: ______________________________

© 2018 Cengage. May not be scanned, copied or duplicated, or posted to a publicly accessible website, in whole or in part.

EXERCISE 23-14, Concluded

Step 3: ______________________

© 2018 Cengage. May not be scanned, copied or duplicated, or posted to a publicly accessible website, in whole or in part.

EXERCISE 23-15

	A	B	C	D
1	LENO MANUFACTURING COMPANY			
2	Factory Overhead Cost Budget—Press Department			
3	For the Month Ended November 30			
4				
5				
6				
7				
8				
9				
10				
11				
12				
13				
14				
15				
16				
17				
18				
19				
20				
21				
22				
23				
24				

© 2018 Cengage. May not be scanned, copied or duplicated, or posted to a publicly accessible website, in whole or in part.

EXERCISE 23-16

a.

	A	B	C	D
1	**WIKI WIKI COMPANY**			
2	**Monthly Factory Overhead Cost Budget—Fabrication Department**			
3				
4				
5				
6				
7				
8				
9				

b. Overhead applied to actual production:

Computations:

© 2018 Cengage. May not be scanned, copied or duplicated, or posted to a publicly accessible website, in whole or in part.

EXERCISE 23-17

Variable factory overhead controllable variance:

Fixed factory overhead volume variance:

Total factory overhead cost variance:

© 2018 Cengage. May not be scanned, copied or duplicated, or posted to a publicly accessible website, in whole or in part.

EXERCISE 23-17, Concluded

Alternative Computation of Overhead Variances:

© 2018 Cengage. May not be scanned, copied or duplicated, or posted to a publicly accessible website, in whole or in part.

EXERCISE 23-18

a. Controllable variance:

b. Volume variance:

Total factory overhead cost variance:

© 2018 Cengage. May not be scanned, copied or duplicated, or posted to a publicly accessible website, in whole or in part.

EXERCISE 23-18, Concluded

Alternative Computation of Overhead Variances:

© 2018 Cengage. May not be scanned, copied or duplicated, or posted to a publicly accessible website, in whole or in part.

Name ______________________________

EXERCISE 23-19

Correct Determination of Factory Overhead Cost Variances:

© 2018 Cengage. May not be scanned, copied or duplicated, or posted to a publicly accessible website, in whole or in part.

EXERCISE 23-19, Concluded

Alternative Computation of Overhead Variances:

© 2018 Cengage. May not be scanned, copied or duplicated, or posted to a publicly accessible website, in whole or in part.

EXERCISE 23-20

	A	B	C	D	E
1	TANNIN PRODUCTS INC.				
2	Factory Overhead Cost Variance Report—Trim Department				
3	For the Month Ended July 31				
4	Productive capacity for the month				
5	Actual productive capacity used for the month				
6					
7					
8			Budget (at actual	Variances	
9		Actual	production)	Unfavorable	Favorable
10					
11					
12					
13					
14					
15					
16					
17					
18					
19					
20					
21					
22					
23					
24					
25					
26					
27					
28					
29					
30					
31					
32					
33					
34					
35					
36					
37					
38					
39					
40					
41					
42					
43					
44					
45					

© 2018 Cengage. May not be scanned, copied or duplicated, or posted to a publicly accessible website, in whole or in part.

EXERCISE 23-20, Continued

Computations:

© 2018 Cengage. May not be scanned, copied or duplicated, or posted to a publicly accessible website, in whole or in part.

EXERCISE 23-20, Concluded

Alternative Computation of Overhead Variances:

© 2018 Cengage. May not be scanned, copied or duplicated, or posted to a publicly accessible website, in whole or in part.

EXERCISE 23-21

a. and b.

JOURNAL PAGE

	DATE		DESCRIPTION	POST. REF.	DEBIT	CREDIT	
1							1
2							2
3							3
4							4
5							5
6							6
7							7
8							8
9							9
10							10
11							11
12							12
13							13
14							14
15							15
16							16

EXERCISE 23-22

JOURNAL PAGE

	DATE		DESCRIPTION	POST. REF.	DEBIT	CREDIT	
1							1
2							2
3							3
4							4
5							5
6							6
7							7
8							8
9							9
10							10
11							11
12							12
13							13
14							14

© 2018 Cengage. May not be scanned, copied or duplicated, or posted to a publicly accessible website, in whole or in part.

EXERCISE 23-23

Income Statement

	UNFAVORABLE	FAVORABLE	

© 2018 Cengage. May not be scanned, copied or duplicated, or posted to a publicly accessible website, in whole or in part.

EXERCISE 23-24

a. and b.

	Input Measure	Output Measure	Explanation
Average computer response time to customer "clicks"			
Dollar amount of returned goods			
Elapsed time between customer order and product delivery			
Maintenance dollars divided by hardware investment			
Number of customer complaints divided by the number of orders			
Number of misfilled orders divided by the number of orders			
Number of orders per warehouse employee			
Number of page faults or errors due to software programming errors			
Number of software fixes per week			
Server (computer) downtime			
Training dollars per programmer			

© 2018 Cengage. May not be scanned, copied or duplicated, or posted to a publicly accessible website, in whole or in part.

Name ______________________________

EXERCISE 23-25

a. Input Measures: ______________________________

Output Measures: ______________________________

b. ______________________________

© 2018 Cengage. May not be scanned, copied or duplicated, or posted to a publicly accessible website, in whole or in part.

This Page Not Used.

© 2018 Cengage. May not be scanned, copied or duplicated, or posted to a publicly accessible website, in whole or in part.

PROBLEM 23-1 ___

a.

b. **Direct Materials Cost Variance**

Price variance: ____________________

Quantity variance: ____________________

Total direct materials cost variance: ____________________

© 2018 Cengage. May not be scanned, copied or duplicated, or posted to a publicly accessible website, in whole or in part.

PROBLEM 23-1 ___, Concluded

c. **Direct Labor Cost Variance**

Rate variance: ______________________

Time variance: ______________________

Total direct labor cost variance: ______________________

© 2018 Cengage. May not be scanned, copied or duplicated, or posted to a publicly accessible website, in whole or in part.

PROBLEM 23-2 ___

1. a.

			TOTAL

© 2018 Cengage. May not be scanned, copied or duplicated, or posted to a publicly accessible website, in whole or in part.

PROBLEM 23-2 ___, Continued

b.

			TOTAL

© 2018 Cengage. May not be scanned, copied or duplicated, or posted to a publicly accessible website, in whole or in part.

PROBLEM 23-2 ___, Concluded

2. ______________________________

© 2018 Cengage. May not be scanned, copied or duplicated, or posted to a publicly accessible website, in whole or in part.

This Page Not Used.

© 2018 Cengage. May not be scanned, copied or duplicated, or posted to a publicly accessible website, in whole or in part.

PROBLEM 23-3 ___

a. **Direct Materials Cost Variance**

Price variance: ______________________________

Quantity variance: ______________________________

Total direct materials cost variance: ______________________________

© 2018 Cengage. May not be scanned, copied or duplicated, or posted to a publicly accessible website, in whole or in part.

PROBLEM 23-3 ___, Continued

b. **Direct Labor Cost Variance**

Rate variance: ____

Time variance: ____

Total direct labor cost variance: ______________________________

© 2018 Cengage. May not be scanned, copied or duplicated, or posted to a publicly accessible website, in whole or in part.

PROBLEM 23-3 ___, Continued

c. **Factory Overhead Cost Variance**

© 2018 Cengage. May not be scanned, copied or duplicated, or posted to a publicly accessible website, in whole or in part.

PROBLEM 23-3 ___, Concluded

Alternative Computation of Overhead Variances:

© 2018 Cengage. May not be scanned, copied or duplicated, or posted to a publicly accessible website, in whole or in part.

PROBLEM 23-4 ___

	A	B	C	D	E
1					
2	Factory Overhead Cost Variance Report—_________ Department				
3					
4	Normal capacity for the month				
5	Actual production for the month				
6					
7				Variances	
8		Actual	Budget	Unfavorable	Favorable
9					
10					
11					
12					
13					
14					
15					
16					
17					
18					
19					
20					
21					
22					
23					
24					
25					
26					
27					
28					
29					
30					
31					
32					
33					
34					
35					
36					
37					
38					
39					
40					

© 2018 Cengage. May not be scanned, copied or duplicated, or posted to a publicly accessible website, in whole or in part.

PROBLEM 23-4 ___, Continued

Computations:

© 2018 Cengage. May not be scanned, copied or duplicated, or posted to a publicly accessible website, in whole or in part.

Name ______________________________

PROBLEM 23-4 ___, Concluded

Alternative Computation of Overhead Variances:

© 2018 Cengage. May not be scanned, copied or duplicated, or posted to a publicly accessible website, in whole or in part.

This Page Not Used.

© 2018 Cengage. May not be scanned, copied or duplicated, or posted to a publicly accessible website, in whole or in part.

PROBLEM 23-5 ___

1.

2.

3.

© 2018 Cengage. May not be scanned, copied or duplicated, or posted to a publicly accessible website, in whole or in part.

PROBLEM 23-5 ___, Continued

4.

5.

© 2018 Cengage. May not be scanned, copied or duplicated, or posted to a publicly accessible website, in whole or in part.

PROBLEM 23-5 ___, Concluded

6. ____

© 2018 Cengage. May not be scanned, copied or duplicated, or posted to a publicly accessible website, in whole or in part.

This Page Not Used.

© 2018 Cengage. May not be scanned, copied or duplicated, or posted to a publicly accessible website, in whole or in part.

COMPREHENSIVE PROBLEM 5

Part A

1.

2.

3.

4.

© 2018 Cengage. May not be scanned, copied or duplicated, or posted to a publicly accessible website, in whole or in part.

COMPREHENSIVE PROBLEM 5, Continued

Part B

5.

Production Budget

	CASES

6.

Direct Materials Purchases Budget

	CREAM BASE (OZ.)	NATURAL OILS (OZ.)	BOTTLES (BOTTLES)	TOTAL

© 2018 Cengage. May not be scanned, copied or duplicated, or posted to a publicly accessible website, in whole or in part.

COMPREHENSIVE PROBLEM 5, Continued

7.

Direct Labor Cost Budget

	MIXING	FILLING	TOTAL

8.

Factory Overhead Cost Budget

© 2018 Cengage. May not be scanned, copied or duplicated, or posted to a publicly accessible website, in whole or in part.

COMPREHENSIVE PROBLEM 5, Continued

9.

Budgeted Income Statement

© 2018 Cengage. May not be scanned, copied or duplicated, or posted to a publicly accessible website, in whole or in part.

COMPREHENSIVE PROBLEM 5, Continued

Part C

10. Direct Materials Price Variance:

	CREAM BASE	NATURAL OILS	BOTTLES

© 2018 Cengage. May not be scanned, copied or duplicated, or posted to a publicly accessible website, in whole or in part.

COMPREHENSIVE PROBLEM 5, Continued

Direct Materials Quantity Variance:

	CREAM BASE	NATURAL OILS	BOTTLES

© 2018 Cengage. May not be scanned, copied or duplicated, or posted to a publicly accessible website, in whole or in part.

COMPREHENSIVE PROBLEM 5, Continued

11. Direct Labor Rate Variance:

	MIXING DEPARTMENT	FILLING DEPARTMENT

© 2018 Cengage. May not be scanned, copied or duplicated, or posted to a publicly accessible website, in whole or in part.

COMPREHENSIVE PROBLEM 5, Continued

Direct Labor Time Variance:

	MIXING DEPARTMENT	FILLING DEPARTMENT

© 2018 Cengage. May not be scanned, copied or duplicated, or posted to a publicly accessible website, in whole or in part.

COMPREHENSIVE PROBLEM 5, Continued

12. Factory Overhead Controllable Variance:

13. Factory Overhead Volume Variance:

© 2018 Cengage. May not be scanned, copied or duplicated, or posted to a publicly accessible website, in whole or in part.

COMPREHENSIVE PROBLEM 5, Continued

Alternative Computation of Overhead Variances:

© 2018 Cengage. May not be scanned, copied or duplicated, or posted to a publicly accessible website, in whole or in part.

COMPREHENSIVE PROBLEM 5, Concluded

14. ____________________

© 2018 Cengage. May not be scanned, copied or duplicated, or posted to a publicly accessible website, in whole or in part.

This Page Not Used.

© 2018 Cengage. May not be scanned, copied or duplicated, or posted to a publicly accessible website, in whole or in part.

EXERCISE 24-1

a.

Garland Company
Budget Performance Report—Vice President, Production
For the Month Ended November 30

Plant	Actual	Budget	Over Budget	Under Budget
Eastern Region	$2,409,400	$2,420,000		$(10,600)
Central Region	2,998,400	3,000,000		(1,600)
Western Region	(g) ________	(h) ________	(i) $ ________	________
	(j) $ ________	(k) $ ________	(l) $ ________	$(12,200)

Garland Company
Budget Performance Report—Manager, Western Region Plant
For the Month Ended November 30

Department	Actual	Budget	Over Budget	Under Budget
Chip Fabrication	(a) $ ________	(b) $ ________	(c) $ ________	
Electronic Assembly	703,200	700,000	3,200	
Final Assembly	516,600	525,000	________	$(8,400)
	(d) $ ________	(e) $ ________	(f) $ ________	$(8,400)

Garland Company
Budget Performance Report—Supervisor, Chip Fabrication
For the Month Ended November 30

Cost	Actual	Budget	Over Budget	Under Budget
Factory wages	$ 95,500	$ 82,000	$13,500	
Materials	115,300	120,000		$(4,700)
Power and light	49,950	45,000	4,950	
Maintenance	37,200	28,000	9,200	________
	$297,950	$275,000	$27,650	$(4,700)

© 2018 Cengage. May not be scanned, copied or duplicated, or posted to a publicly accessible website, in whole or in part.

EXERCISE 24-1, Concluded

b.

EXERCISE 24-2

Divisional Income Statements

	COMMERCIAL DIVISION	RESIDENTIAL DIVISION

© 2018 Cengage. May not be scanned, copied or duplicated, or posted to a publicly accessible website, in whole or in part.

Name ______________________________

EXERCISE 24-3

a. Legal: ______________________________

b. Duplication services: ______________________________

c. Information Technology Help Desk: ______________________________

d. Central purchasing: ______________________________

e. Networking: ______________________________

f. Accounts receivable: ______________________________

EXERCISE 24-4

a. Accounts Receivable: ______________________________

b. Central Purchasing: ______________________________

c. Computer Support: ______________________________

d. Conferences: ______________________________

e. Employee Travel: ______________________________

f. Payroll Accounting: ______________________________

g. Telecommunications: ______________________________

h. Training: ______________________________

EXERCISE 24-5

a.

	RESIDENTIAL	COMMERCIAL	GOVERNMENT CONTRACT	TOTAL

© 2018 Cengage. May not be scanned, copied or duplicated, or posted to a publicly accessible website, in whole or in part.

EXERCISE 24-5, Continued

b.

	RESIDENTIAL	COMMERCIAL	GOVERNMENT CONTRACT	TOTAL

© 2018 Cengage. May not be scanned, copied or duplicated, or posted to a publicly accessible website, in whole or in part.

EXERCISE 24-5, Concluded

c. ____________________

EXERCISE 24-6

a. Help desk: ______________________

Network center: ______________________

Electronic mail: ______________________

Handheld Technology support: ______________________

b. Help desk: ______________________

Network center: ______________________

Electronic mail: ______________________

Handheld Technology support: ______________________

© 2018 Cengage. May not be scanned, copied or duplicated, or posted to a publicly accessible website, in whole or in part.

EXERCISE 24-7

Divisional Income Statements

	CONSUMER DIVISION		COMMERCIAL DIVISION	

Supporting calculations:

© 2018 Cengage. May not be scanned, copied or duplicated, or posted to a publicly accessible website, in whole or in part.

EXERCISE 24-8

a. ____________________

© 2018 Cengage. May not be scanned, copied or duplicated, or posted to a publicly accessible website, in whole or in part.

EXERCISE 24-8, Concluded

b.

Divisional Income Statements

	PASSENGER DIVISION		CARGO DIVISION	

Supporting calculations:

© 2018 Cengage. May not be scanned, copied or duplicated, or posted to a publicly accessible website, in whole or in part.

EXERCISE 24-9

Divisional Income Statements

	WINTER SPORTS DIVISION	SUMMER SPORTS DIVISION

© 2018 Cengage. May not be scanned, copied or duplicated, or posted to a publicly accessible website, in whole or in part.

EXERCISE 24-9, Concluded

Supporting calculations:

© 2018 Cengage. May not be scanned, copied or duplicated, or posted to a publicly accessible website, in whole or in part.

EXERCISE 24-10

a. Retail Division: ______________________

Commercial Division: ______________________

Internet Division: ______________________

b. ______________________

EXERCISE 24-11

a.

	RETAIL DIVISION	COMMERCIAL DIVISION	INTERNET DIVISION

b. ______________________

EXERCISE 24-12

Return on Investment	=	Profit Margin	×	Investment Turnover
13.2%	=	6%	×	**(a)** __________
(b) __________	=	10%	×	1.80
10.5%	=	**(c)** __________	×	1.50
15.0%	=	5%	×	**(d)** __________
(e) __________	=	12%	×	1.10

© 2018 Cengage. May not be scanned, copied or duplicated, or posted to a publicly accessible website, in whole or in part.

EXERCISE 24-13

a.

b.

© 2018 Cengage. May not be scanned, copied or duplicated, or posted to a publicly accessible website, in whole or in part.

EXERCISE 24-14

a. ____

Media Networks: ____

Parks and Resorts: ____

Studio Entertainment: ____

Consumer Products: ____

© 2018 Cengage. May not be scanned, copied or duplicated, or posted to a publicly accessible website, in whole or in part.

EXERCISE 24-14, Concluded

b.

© 2018 Cengage. May not be scanned, copied or duplicated, or posted to a publicly accessible website, in whole or in part.

EXERCISE 24-15

Invested Assets	Income from Operations	Return on Investment	Minimum Return	Minimum Acceptable Income from Operations	Residual Income
$925,000	$185,000	(a) ________	15%	(b) $________	(c) $________
$775,000	(d) $________	(e) ________	(f) ________	$93,000	$23,250
$450,000	(g) $________	18%	(h) ________	$58,500	(i) $________
$610,000	$97,600	(j) ________	12%	(k) $________	(l) $________

Calculations:

(a) ____________________

(b) ____________________

(c) ____________________

(d) ____________________

(e) ____________________

(f) ____________________

(g) ____________________

(h) ____________________

(i) ____________________

(j) ____________________

(k) ____________________

(l) ____________________

© 2018 Cengage. May not be scanned, copied or duplicated, or posted to a publicly accessible website, in whole or in part.

EXERCISE 24-16

a.

	Sales	Income from Operations	Invested Assets	Return on Investment	Profit Margin	Investment Turnover
North	$860,000	**(a)** $______	**(b)** $______	17.5%	7.0%	**(c)** ______
South	**(d)** $______	$51,300	**(e)** $______	**(f)** ______	4.5%	3.8
East	$1,020,000	**(g)** $______	$680,000	15.0%	**(h)** ______	**(i)** ______
West	$1,120,000	$89,600	$560,000	**(j)** ______	**(k)** ______	**(l)** ______

Calculations:

(a) ______

(b) ______

(c) ______

(d) ______

(e) ______

(f) ______

(g) ______

(h) ______

(i) ______

(j) ______

(k) ______

(l) ______

b. North Division: ______

South Division: ______

East Division: ______

West Division: ______

c. **(1)** ______

(2) ______

© 2018 Cengage. May not be scanned, copied or duplicated, or posted to a publicly accessible website, in whole or in part.

EXERCISE 24-17

a. ______________________

Company-Owned: ______________________

Franchised Operations: ______________________

b.

	COMPANY-OWNED	FRANCHISED OPERATIONS

© 2018 Cengage. May not be scanned, copied or duplicated, or posted to a publicly accessible website, in whole or in part.

EXERCISE 24-17, Concluded

c.

© 2018 Cengage. May not be scanned, copied or duplicated, or posted to a publicly accessible website, in whole or in part.

EXERCISE 24-18

Average card member spending: ______________________

____

Cards in force: ______________________

____

Earnings growth: ______________________

____

Hours of credit consultant training: ______________________

____

Investment in information technology: ______________________

____

Number of card choices: ______________________

____

Number of Internet features: ______________________

____

Number of merchant signings: ______________________

____

Number of new card launches: ______________________

____

Return on equity: ______________________

____

Revenue growth: ______________________

____

© 2018 Cengage. May not be scanned, copied or duplicated, or posted to a publicly accessible website, in whole or in part.

EXERCISE 24-19

© 2018 Cengage. May not be scanned, copied or duplicated, or posted to a publicly accessible website, in whole or in part.

EXERCISE 24-20

a.

b.

c.

© 2018 Cengage. May not be scanned, copied or duplicated, or posted to a publicly accessible website, in whole or in part.

EXERCISE 24-21

a.

b.

c.

© 2018 Cengage. May not be scanned, copied or duplicated, or posted to a publicly accessible website, in whole or in part.

EXERCISE 24-21, Concluded

d. ____

© 2018 Cengage. May not be scanned, copied or duplicated, or posted to a publicly accessible website, in whole or in part.

Name ______________________________

PROBLEM 24-1 ___

1.

Budget Performance Report — ____________________

	ACTUAL	BUDGET	OVER BUDGET	UNDER BUDGET

2. ______________________________

© 2018 Cengage. May not be scanned, copied or duplicated, or posted to a publicly accessible website, in whole or in part.

This Page Not Used.

© 2018 Cengage. May not be scanned, copied or duplicated, or posted to a publicly accessible website, in whole or in part.

PROBLEM 24-2 ___

1.

Divisional Income Statements

© 2018 Cengage. May not be scanned, copied or duplicated, or posted to a publicly accessible website, in whole or in part.

PROBLEM 24-2 ___, Continued

Supporting calculations:

© 2018 Cengage. May not be scanned, copied or duplicated, or posted to a publicly accessible website, in whole or in part.

PROBLEM 24-2 ___, Continued

2. ____

© 2018 Cengage. May not be scanned, copied or duplicated, or posted to a publicly accessible website, in whole or in part.

PROBLEM 24-2 ___, Concluded

3. ______________________

© 2018 Cengage. May not be scanned, copied or duplicated, or posted to a publicly accessible website, in whole or in part.

PROBLEM 24-3 ___

1.

Divisional Income Statements

© 2018 Cengage. May not be scanned, copied or duplicated, or posted to a publicly accessible website, in whole or in part.

PROBLEM 24-3 ___, Continued

2.

© 2018 Cengage. May not be scanned, copied or duplicated, or posted to a publicly accessible website, in whole or in part.

PROBLEM 24-4 ___

1. ____________________

PROBLEM 24-4 ___, Continued

2.

Estimated Income Statements

	PROPOSAL 1	PROPOSAL 2	PROPOSAL 3

© 2018 Cengage. May not be scanned, copied or duplicated, or posted to a publicly accessible website, in whole or in part.

PROBLEM 24-4 ___, Continued

3. ______________________________

4. ______________________________

© 2018 Cengage. May not be scanned, copied or duplicated, or posted to a publicly accessible website, in whole or in part.

PROBLEM 24-4 ___, Concluded

5. ______________________________

© 2018 Cengage. May not be scanned, copied or duplicated, or posted to a publicly accessible website, in whole or in part.

PROBLEM 24-5 ___

1.

Divisional Income Statements

© 2018 Cengage. May not be scanned, copied or duplicated, or posted to a publicly accessible website, in whole or in part.

PROBLEM 24-5 ___, Continued

2. ______________________

3. ______________________

© 2018 Cengage. May not be scanned, copied or duplicated, or posted to a publicly accessible website, in whole or in part.

PROBLEM 24-5 ___, Concluded

4. ______________________

© 2018 Cengage. May not be scanned, copied or duplicated, or posted to a publicly accessible website, in whole or in part.

This Page Not Used.

© 2018 Cengage. May not be scanned, copied or duplicated, or posted to a publicly accessible website, in whole or in part.

PROBLEM 24-6 ___

1. ____________________

____

____

____

____

© 2018 Cengage. May not be scanned, copied or duplicated, or posted to a publicly accessible website, in whole or in part.

PROBLEM 24-6 ___, Continued

2. Increase in ______________ Division's income from operations: ______________________

____

____

____

Increase in ______________ Division's income from operations: ______________________

____

____

____

Increase in company's total income from operations: ______________________

____

____

____

© 2018 Cengage. May not be scanned, copied or duplicated, or posted to a publicly accessible website, in whole or in part.

PROBLEM 24-6 ___, Continued

3.

Divisional Income Statements

			TOTAL

© 2018 Cengage. May not be scanned, copied or duplicated, or posted to a publicly accessible website, in whole or in part.

PROBLEM 24-6 ___, Continued

4. Increase in _____________ Division's income from operations: _______________________

Increase in _____________ Division's income from operations: _______________________

Increase in company's total income from operations: _______________________

© 2018 Cengage. May not be scanned, copied or duplicated, or posted to a publicly accessible website, in whole or in part.

PROBLEM 24-6 ___, Concluded

5. a. ____

____

____

____

____

b. ____

____

____

____

____

____

____

____

____

____

© 2018 Cengage. May not be scanned, copied or duplicated, or posted to a publicly accessible website, in whole or in part.

This Page Not Used.

© 2018 Cengage. May not be scanned, copied or duplicated, or posted to a publicly accessible website, in whole or in part.

EXERCISE 25-1

a.

Lease Machinery (Alternative 1) or Sell Machinery (Alternative 2)

	LEASE MACHINERY (ALTERNATIVE 1)	SELL MACHINERY (ALTERNATIVE 2)	DIFFERENTIAL EFFECT ON INCOME (ALTERNATIVE 2)

b. ______________________

EXERCISE 25-2

Lease Equipment (Alternative 1) or Buy Equipment (Alternative 2)

	LEASE EQUIPMENT (ALTERNATIVE 1)	BUY EQUIPMENT (ALTERNATIVE 2)	DIFFERENTIAL EFFECT ON INCOME (ALTERNATIVE 2)

© 2018 Cengage. May not be scanned, copied or duplicated, or posted to a publicly accessible website, in whole or in part.

EXERCISE 25-3

a.

Continue Star Cola (Alternative 1) or Discontinue Star Cola (Alternative 2)

	CONTINUE STAR COLA (ALTERNATIVE 1)	DISCONTINUE STAR COLA (ALTERNATIVE 2)	DIFFERENTIAL EFFECT ON INCOME (ALTERNATIVE 2)

b. ______________________________

____

____

____

© 2018 Cengage. May not be scanned, copied or duplicated, or posted to a publicly accessible website, in whole or in part.

EXERCISE 25-4

a.

Continue Cups (Alternative 1) or Discontinue Cups (Alternative 2)

	CONTINUE CUPS (ALTERNATIVE 1)	DISCONTINUE CUPS (ALTERNATIVE 2)	DIFFERENTIAL EFFECT ON INCOME (ALTERNATIVE 2)

b. ____________________

© 2018 Cengage. May not be scanned, copied or duplicated, or posted to a publicly accessible website, in whole or in part.

EXERCISE 25-5

a.

b.

c.

	INVESTOR SERVICES (IN MILLIONS)	ADVISOR SERVICES (IN MILLIONS)

© 2018 Cengage. May not be scanned, copied or duplicated, or posted to a publicly accessible website, in whole or in part.

EXERCISE 25-5, Concluded

d.

EXERCISE 25-6

Continue Children's Shoes (Alternative 1) or Discontinue Children's Shoes (Alternative 2)			
	CONTINUE CHILDREN'S SHOES (ALTERNATIVE 1)	DISCONTINUE CHILDREN'S SHOES (ALTERNATIVE 2)	DIFFERENTIAL EFFECT ON INCOME (ALTERNATIVE 2)

© 2018 Cengage. May not be scanned, copied or duplicated, or posted to a publicly accessible website, in whole or in part.

EXERCISE 25-7

a.

Make Carrying Case (Alternative 1) or Buy Carrying Case (Alternative 2)

	MAKE CARRYING CASE (ALTERNATIVE 1)	BUY CARRYING CASE (ALTERNATIVE 2)	DIFFERENTIAL EFFECT ON INCOME (ALTERNATIVE 2)

b. ______________________________

© 2018 Cengage. May not be scanned, copied or duplicated, or posted to a publicly accessible website, in whole or in part.

Name ______________________________

EXERCISE 25-8

a.

Lay Out Pages Internally (Alternative 1) or Purchase Layout Services (Alternative 2)

	LAY OUT PAGES INTERNALLY (ALTERNATIVE 1)	PURCHASE LAYOUT SERVICES (ALTERNATIVE 2)	DIFFERENTIAL EFFECT ON INCOME (ALTERNATIVE 2)

b. ______________________________

© 2018 Cengage. May not be scanned, copied or duplicated, or posted to a publicly accessible website, in whole or in part.

EXERCISE 25-8, Concluded

c.

EXERCISE 25-9

a.

Continue with Old Machine (Alternative 1) or Replace Old Machine (Alternative 2)

	CONTINUE WITH OLD MACHINE (ALTERNATIVE 1)	REPLACE OLD MACHINE (ALTERNATIVE 2)	DIFFERENTIAL EFFECT ON INCOME (ALTERNATIVE 2)

b.

© 2018 Cengage. May not be scanned, copied or duplicated, or posted to a publicly accessible website, in whole or in part.

EXERCISE 25-10

a.

Continue with Old Machine (Alternative 1) or Replace Old Machine (Alternative 2)

	CONTINUE WITH OLD MACHINE (ALTERNATIVE 1)	REPLACE OLD MACHINE (ALTERNATIVE 2)	DIFFERENTIAL EFFECT ON INCOME (ALTERNATIVE 2)

b. ______________________

c. ______________________

© 2018 Cengage. May not be scanned, copied or duplicated, or posted to a publicly accessible website, in whole or in part.

EXERCISE 25-11

Sell Rough Cut (Alternative 1) or Process Further into Finished Cut (Alternative 2)

	SELL ROUGH CUT (ALTERNATIVE 1)	PROCESS FURTHER INTO FINISHED CUT (ALTERNATIVE 2)	DIFFERENTIAL EFFECT ON INCOME (ALTERNATIVE 2)

EXERCISE 25-12

a.

Sell Regular Columbian (Alternative 1) or Process Further into Decaf Columbian (Alternative 2)

	SELL REGULAR COLUMBIAN (ALTERNATIVE 1)	PROCESS FURTHER INTO DECAF COLUMBIAN (ALTERNATIVE 2)	DIFFERENTIAL EFFECT ON INCOME (ALTERNATIVE 2)

b. ______________________________

© 2018 Cengage. May not be scanned, copied or duplicated, or posted to a publicly accessible website, in whole or in part.

EXERCISE 25-12, Concluded

c.

Sell Regular Columbian (Alternative 1) or Process Further into Decaf Columbian (Alternative 2)

	SELL REGULAR COLUMBIAN (ALTERNATIVE 1)	PROCESS FURTHER INTO DECAF COLUMBIAN (ALTERNATIVE 2)	DIFFERENTIAL EFFECT ON INCOME (ALTERNATIVE 2)

© 2018 Cengage. May not be scanned, copied or duplicated, or posted to a publicly accessible website, in whole or in part.

EXERCISE 25-13

a.

Reject Order (Alternative 1) or Accept Order (Alternative 2)

	REJECT ORDER (ALTERNATIVE 1)	ACCEPT ORDER (ALTERNATIVE 2)	DIFFERENTIAL EFFECT ON INCOME (ALTERNATIVE 2)

b.

c.

EXERCISE 25-14

© 2018 Cengage. May not be scanned, copied or duplicated, or posted to a publicly accessible website, in whole or in part.

Name ______________________________

EXERCISE 25-15

a.

Reject Order (Alternative 1) or Accept Order (Alternative 2)

	REJECT ORDER (ALTERNATIVE 1)	ACCEPT ORDER (ALTERNATIVE 2)	DIFFERENTIAL EFFECT ON INCOME (ALTERNATIVE 2)

b. ______________________________

© 2018 Cengage. May not be scanned, copied or duplicated, or posted to a publicly accessible website, in whole or in part.

EXERCISE 25-16

a.

b. ______________________

© 2018 Cengage. May not be scanned, copied or duplicated, or posted to a publicly accessible website, in whole or in part.

EXERCISE 25-17

a. ____________________

b. ____________________

c. ____________________

d.

EXERCISE 25-18

a. ____________________

b. ____________________

c. ____________________

© 2018 Cengage. May not be scanned, copied or duplicated, or posted to a publicly accessible website, in whole or in part.

EXERCISE 25-18, Concluded

d.

EXERCISE 25-19

a. ______________________

b. ______________________

© 2018 Cengage. May not be scanned, copied or duplicated, or posted to a publicly accessible website, in whole or in part.

Name ____________________

EXERCISE 25-20

a. ____________________

b. ____________________

c.

© 2018 Cengage. May not be scanned, copied or duplicated, or posted to a publicly accessible website, in whole or in part.

EXERCISE 25-21

	TYPE 5	TYPE 10	TYPE 20

© 2018 Cengage. May not be scanned, copied or duplicated, or posted to a publicly accessible website, in whole or in part.

EXERCISE 25-22

a.

	LARGE	MEDIUM	SMALL	TOTAL

b. ____

____

	LARGE	MEDIUM	SMALL

© 2018 Cengage. May not be scanned, copied or duplicated, or posted to a publicly accessible website, in whole or in part.

Name ______________________

EXERCISE 25-23

	A	B	C	D	E	F	G	H	I	J	K	L
1		Stationary Bicycle						Treadmill				
2		________	—	________	=	Activity		________	—	________	=	Activity
3	Activity	________		________		Cost		________		________		Cost
4												
5												
6												
7												
8												
9												
10												
11												
12												
13												
14												
15												

© 2018 Cengage. May not be scanned, copied or duplicated, or posted to a publicly accessible website, in whole or in part.

EXERCISE 25-24

a.

	PRODUCTION SETUP	PROCUREMENT	QUALITY CONTROL	MATERIALS MANAGEMENT

b.

	CUSTOM		STANDARD	

© 2018 Cengage. May not be scanned, copied or duplicated, or posted to a publicly accessible website, in whole or in part.

EXERCISE 25-24, Concluded

c. ____

d. ____

© 2018 Cengage. May not be scanned, copied or duplicated, or posted to a publicly accessible website, in whole or in part.

EXERCISE 25-25

a.

	A	B	C	D	E	F
1						Activity
2	Activity		—		=	Rate
3						
4						
5						
6						
7						
8						
9						
10						

b.

	A	B	C	D	E	F	G	H	I	J	K	L
1		Entry Lighting Fixtures										
2						Activity		Dining Room Lighting Fixtures				
3	Activity		—		=	Cost			—		=	Activity Cost
4												
5												
6												
7												
8												
9												
10												
11												
12												
13												
14												
15												

© 2018 Cengage. May not be scanned, copied or duplicated, or posted to a publicly accessible website, in whole or in part.

APPENDIX EXERCISE 25-26

a.

b.

c.

© 2018 Cengage. May not be scanned, copied or duplicated, or posted to a publicly accessible website, in whole or in part.

APPENDIX EXERCISE 25-27

a.

b.

c.

© 2018 Cengage. May not be scanned, copied or duplicated, or posted to a publicly accessible website, in whole or in part.

This Page Not Used.

© 2018 Cengage. May not be scanned, copied or duplicated, or posted to a publicly accessible website, in whole or in part.

Name ______________________________

PROBLEM 25-1 ___

1.

Operate ______________ (Alternative 1) or Invest in Bonds (Alternative 2)

	OPERATE ______ ______ (ALTERNATIVE 1)	INVEST IN BONDS (ALTERNATIVE 2)	DIFFERENTIAL EFFECT ON INCOME (ALTERNATIVE 2)

2. ______________________________

____

3.

© 2018 Cengage. May not be scanned, copied or duplicated, or posted to a publicly accessible website, in whole or in part.

This Page Not Used

© 2018 Cengage. May not be scanned, copied or duplicated, or posted to a publicly accessible website, in whole or in part.

PROBLEM 25-2 ___

1.

Continue with Old Machine (Alternative 1) or Replace Old Machine (Alternative 2)

	CONTINUE WITH OLD MACHINE (ALTERNATIVE 1)	REPLACE OLD MACHINE (ALTERNATIVE 2)	DIFFERENTIAL EFFECT ON INCOME (ALTERNATIVE 2)

© 2018 Cengage. May not be scanned, copied or duplicated, or posted to a publicly accessible website, in whole or in part.

PROBLEM 25-2 ___, Concluded

2. ____________________

© 2018 Cengage. May not be scanned, copied or duplicated, or posted to a publicly accessible website, in whole or in part.

PROBLEM 25-3 ___

1.

Promote ________ (Alternative 1) or Promote ________ (Alternative 2)

	PROMOTE ________ (ALTERNATIVE 1)	PROMOTE ________ (ALTERNATIVE 2)	DIFFERENTIAL EFFECT ON INCOME (ALTERNATIVE 2)

2.

© 2018 Cengage. May not be scanned, copied or duplicated, or posted to a publicly accessible website, in whole or in part.

This Page Not Used.

© 2018 Cengage. May not be scanned, copied or duplicated, or posted to a publicly accessible website, in whole or in part.

PROBLEM 25-4 ___

1.

Sell ______________ (Alternative 1) or Process Further into ______________ (Alternative 2)

	SELL ______ ______ (ALTERNATIVE 1)	PROCESS FURTHER INTO ______ ______ (ALTERNATIVE 2)	DIFFERENTIAL EFFECT ON INCOME (ALTERNATIVE 2)

2. ____

© 2018 Cengage. May not be scanned, copied or duplicated, or posted to a publicly accessible website, in whole or in part.

This Page Not Used.

© 2018 Cengage. May not be scanned, copied or duplicated, or posted to a publicly accessible website, in whole or in part.

PROBLEM 25-5 ___

1. ____________________

2. a.

____

____

b. ____________________

c.

© 2018 Cengage. May not be scanned, copied or duplicated, or posted to a publicly accessible website, in whole or in part.

PROBLEM 25-5 ___, Continued

3. (APPENDIX)

a.

b.

c.

© 2018 Cengage. May not be scanned, copied or duplicated, or posted to a publicly accessible website, in whole or in part.

PROBLEM 25-5 ___, Continued

4. (APPENDIX)

a. ______________________________

b. ______________________________

c.

5. ______________________________

© 2018 Cengage. May not be scanned, copied or duplicated, or posted to a publicly accessible website, in whole or in part.

PROBLEM 25-5 ___, Concluded

6. a.

Reject Order (Alternative 1) or Accept Order (Alternative 2)

	REJECT ORDER (ALTERNATIVE 1)	ACCEPT ORDER (ALTERNATIVE 2)	DIFFERENTIAL EFFECT ON INCOME (ALTERNATIVE 2)

b. ____

____

© 2018 Cengage. May not be scanned, copied or duplicated, or posted to a publicly accessible website, in whole or in part.

PROBLEM 25-6 ___

1.

© 2018 Cengage. May not be scanned, copied or duplicated, or posted to a publicly accessible website, in whole or in part.

PROBLEM 25-6 ___, Concluded

2.

Explanation:

© 2018 Cengage. May not be scanned, copied or duplicated, or posted to a publicly accessible website, in whole or in part.

PROBLEM 25-7 ___

1.

© 2018 Cengage. May not be scanned, copied or duplicated, or posted to a publicly accessible website, in whole or in part.

Name ____________________

PROBLEM 25-7 ____, Continued

2.

	A	B	C	D	E	F	G	H	I	J	K	L
1												
2			—		=	Activity Cost			—		=	Activity Cost
3	Activity											
4												
5												
6												
7												
8												
9												
10												
11												
12												
13												
14												
15												

	A	B	C	D	E	F
1						
2			—		=	Activity Cost
3	Activity					
4						
5						
6						
7						
8						
9						
10						
11						
12						
13						
14						
15						

© 2018 Cengage. May not be scanned, copied or duplicated, or posted to a publicly accessible website, in whole or in part.

PROBLEM 25-7 ___, Concluded

3. ____________________

© 2018 Cengage. May not be scanned, copied or duplicated, or posted to a publicly accessible website, in whole or in part.

This Page Not Used.

© 2018 Cengage. May not be scanned, copied or duplicated, or posted to a publicly accessible website, in whole or in part.

EXERCISE 26-1

	3D PRINTER	TRUCK

EXERCISE 26-2

© 2018 Cengage. May not be scanned, copied or duplicated, or posted to a publicly accessible website, in whole or in part.

EXERCISE 26-3

EXERCISE 26-4

	YEAR 1	YEARS 2–9	LAST YEAR

© 2018 Cengage. May not be scanned, copied or duplicated, or posted to a publicly accessible website, in whole or in part.

EXERCISE 26-5

	NET CASH FLOW	CUMULATIVE NET CASH FLOWS

EXERCISE 26-6

a.

	LIQUID SOAP		BODY LOTION	
	NET CASH FLOW	CUMULATIVE NET CASH FLOWS	NET CASH FLOW	CUMULATIVE NET CASH FLOWS

© 2018 Cengage. May not be scanned, copied or duplicated, or posted to a publicly accessible website, in whole or in part.

EXERCISE 26-6, Concluded

b. ____

EXERCISE 26-7

a.

Year	Present Value of $1 at 15%	Net Cash Flow	Present Value of Net Cash Flow
1			
2			
3			
4			
Total			
Less amount to be invested			
Net present value			

b. ____

© 2018 Cengage. May not be scanned, copied or duplicated, or posted to a publicly accessible website, in whole or in part.

Name ____________________

EXERCISE 26-8

a.

	20Y1	20Y2	20Y3	20Y4	20Y5

b.

Year	Net Cash Flow [from part a.]	Present Value of $1 at 12%	Present Value of Net Cash Flow
20Y1			
20Y2			
20Y3			
20Y4			
20Y5			
Total present value of cash flows			
Less investment in delivery truck			
Net present value of delivery truck			

c. ____________________

© 2018 Cengage. May not be scanned, copied or duplicated, or posted to a publicly accessible website, in whole or in part.

EXERCISE 26-9

a.

	(IN MILLIONS)	

b.

	(IN MILLIONS, EXCEPT PRESENT VALUE FACTOR)

c. ________________________

© 2018 Cengage. May not be scanned, copied or duplicated, or posted to a publicly accessible website, in whole or in part.

Name ______________________

EXERCISE 26-10

a.

b.

c. ______________________

© 2018 Cengage. May not be scanned, copied or duplicated, or posted to a publicly accessible website, in whole or in part.

EXERCISE 26-10, Concluded

d. ______________________

EXERCISE 26-11

a.

b.

EXERCISE 26-12

a. ______________________

© 2018 Cengage. May not be scanned, copied or duplicated, or posted to a publicly accessible website, in whole or in part.

EXERCISE 26-12, Concluded

b. ______________________

EXERCISE 26-13

a. ______________________

Sewing Machine:

Packing Machine:

© 2018 Cengage. May not be scanned, copied or duplicated, or posted to a publicly accessible website, in whole or in part.

EXERCISE 26-13, Concluded

b. ____

c. ____

© 2018 Cengage. May not be scanned, copied or duplicated, or posted to a publicly accessible website, in whole or in part.

EXERCISE 26-14

a.

b.

c.

EXERCISE 26-15

a.

b.

© 2018 Cengage. May not be scanned, copied or duplicated, or posted to a publicly accessible website, in whole or in part.

EXERCISE 26-15, Concluded

c. ____

© 2018 Cengage. May not be scanned, copied or duplicated, or posted to a publicly accessible website, in whole or in part.

EXERCISE 26-16

a. ______________________________

____

____

____

____

____

____

b. ______________________________

____

© 2018 Cengage. May not be scanned, copied or duplicated, or posted to a publicly accessible website, in whole or in part.

EXERCISE 26-17

a.

b.

© 2018 Cengage. May not be scanned, copied or duplicated, or posted to a publicly accessible website, in whole or in part.

EXERCISE 26-18

a. Delivery Truck:

Bagging Machine:

© 2018 Cengage. May not be scanned, copied or duplicated, or posted to a publicly accessible website, in whole or in part.

EXERCISE 26-18, Concluded

b.

EXERCISE 26-19

a.

b.

c.

© 2018 Cengage. May not be scanned, copied or duplicated, or posted to a publicly accessible website, in whole or in part.

Name ______________________________

EXERCISE 26-20

© 2018 Cengage. May not be scanned, copied or duplicated, or posted to a publicly accessible website, in whole or in part.

EXERCISE 26-21

Processing Mill:

Year	Present Value of $1 at 15%	Net Cash Flow	Present Value of Net Cash Flow
1			
2			
3			
4			
4 (residual value)			
Total			
Less amount to be invested			
Net present value			

Electric Shovel:

Year	Present Value of $1 at 15%	Net Cash Flow	Present Value of Net Cash Flow
1			
2			
3			
4			
Total			
Less amount to be invested			
Net present value			

Conclusion with explanation:

____

____

____

____

____

____

____

© 2018 Cengage. May not be scanned, copied or duplicated, or posted to a publicly accessible website, in whole or in part.

Name ______________________________

EXERCISE 26-22

a. Blending Equipment:

Computer System:

b. ______________________________

© 2018 Cengage. May not be scanned, copied or duplicated, or posted to a publicly accessible website, in whole or in part.

EXERCISE 26-23

a.

b.

c.

© 2018 Cengage. May not be scanned, copied or duplicated, or posted to a publicly accessible website, in whole or in part.

Name ______________________________

EXERCISE 26-24

a.

	SILICA-BLENDED TIRES

b.

c.

© 2018 Cengage. May not be scanned, copied or duplicated, or posted to a publicly accessible website, in whole or in part.

This Page Not Used.

© 2018 Cengage. May not be scanned, copied or duplicated, or posted to a publicly accessible website, in whole or in part.

PROBLEM 26-1 ___

1\. a. ______________________________

b.

Year	Present Value of $1 at _____%	Net Cash Flow		Present Value of Net Cash Flow	
		Project:	Project:	Project:	Project:
1					
2					
3					
4					
5					
Total...............................					
Less amount to be invested..					
Net present value					

2\. ______________________________

© 2018 Cengage. May not be scanned, copied or duplicated, or posted to a publicly accessible website, in whole or in part.

This Page Not Used.

© 2018 Cengage. May not be scanned, copied or duplicated, or posted to a publicly accessible website, in whole or in part.

Name ______________________________

PROBLEM 26-2 ___

1. a.

____

Year	Net Cash Flow	Cumulative Net Cash Flow

____

Year	Net Cash Flow	Cumulative Net Cash Flow

b.

Year	Present Value of $1 at _____%	Net Cash Flow		Present Value of Net Cash Flow	
		Project (Product): ____ ____	Project (Product): ____ ____	Project (Product): ____ ____	Project (Product): ____ ____
1					
2					
3					
4					
5					
Total................................					
Less amount to be invested..........					
Net present value					

© 2018 Cengage. May not be scanned, copied or duplicated, or posted to a publicly accessible website, in whole or in part.

PROBLEM 26-2 ___, Concluded

2. ______________________________

© 2018 Cengage. May not be scanned, copied or duplicated, or posted to a publicly accessible website, in whole or in part.

PROBLEM 26-3 ___

1. Proposal (Project): ______________________

Year	Present Value of $1 at _____%	Net Cash Flow	Present Value of Net Cash Flow
1			
2			
3			
Total			
Less amount to be invested			
Net present value			

Proposal (Project): ______________________

Year	Present Value of $1 at _____%	Net Cash Flow	Present Value of Net Cash Flow
1			
2			
3			
Total			
Less amount to be invested			
Net present value			

Proposal (Project): ______________________

Year	Present Value of $1 at _____%	Net Cash Flow	Present Value of Net Cash Flow
1			
2			
3			
Total			
Less amount to be invested			
Net present value			

© 2018 Cengage. May not be scanned, copied or duplicated, or posted to a publicly accessible website, in whole or in part.

PROBLEM 26-3 ___, Concluded

2. ____

3. ____

© 2018 Cengage. May not be scanned, copied or duplicated, or posted to a publicly accessible website, in whole or in part.

PROBLEM 26-4 ___

1. a. Project: ______________________________

Project: ______________________________

b. ______________________________

© 2018 Cengage. May not be scanned, copied or duplicated, or posted to a publicly accessible website, in whole or in part.

PROBLEM 26-4 ___, Concluded

2. a. ____

b. ____

3. ____

© 2018 Cengage. May not be scanned, copied or duplicated, or posted to a publicly accessible website, in whole or in part.

Name ______________________________

PROBLEM 26-5 ___

1. Project (Site): ______________________________

Project (Site): ______________________________

2.

Year	Present Value of $1 at _____%	Net Cash Flow		Present Value of Net Cash Flow	
		Project (Site): ________	Project (Site): ________	Project (Site): ________	Project (Site): ________
1					
2					
3					
4					
4 (residual value)					
Total					
Less amount to be invested					
Net present value					

© 2018 Cengage. May not be scanned, copied or duplicated, or posted to a publicly accessible website, in whole or in part.

PROBLEM 26-5 ___, Concluded

3. ____

© 2018 Cengage. May not be scanned, copied or duplicated, or posted to a publicly accessible website, in whole or in part.

PROBLEM 26-6 ___

1. Proposal A:

Year	Net Cash Flow	Cumulative Net Cash Flows

Proposal B:

Year	Net Cash Flow	Cumulative Net Cash Flows

Proposal C:

Year	Net Cash Flow	Cumulative Net Cash Flows

Proposal D:

Year	Net Cash Flow	Cumulative Net Cash Flows

© 2018 Cengage. May not be scanned, copied or duplicated, or posted to a publicly accessible website, in whole or in part.

PROBLEM 26-6 ___, Continued

2. Proposal A: ______________________________

Proposal B: ______________________________

Proposal C: ______________________________

Proposal D: ______________________________

© 2018 Cengage. May not be scanned, copied or duplicated, or posted to a publicly accessible website, in whole or in part.

Name ________________________________

PROBLEM 26-6 ___, Continued

3.

Proposal	Cash Payback Period	Average Rate of Return	Accept for Further Analysis	Reject
A				
B				
C				
D				

4. Proposal ___:

Year	Present Value of $1 at _____%	Net Cash Flow	Present Value of Net Cash Flow
1			
2			
3			
4			
5			
Total........			
Less amount to be invested........			
Net present value			

Proposal ___:

Year	Present Value of $1 at _____%	Net Cash Flow	Present Value of Net Cash Flow
1			
2			
3			
4			
5			
Total........			
Less amount to be invested........			
Net present value			

© 2018 Cengage. May not be scanned, copied or duplicated, or posted to a publicly accessible website, in whole or in part.

PROBLEM 26-6 ___, Concluded

5. ______________________________

6. ______________________________

7. ______________________________

8. ______________________________

© 2018 Cengage. May not be scanned, copied or duplicated, or posted to a publicly accessible website, in whole or in part.

EXTRA FORMS

JOURNAL

PAGE

	DATE		DESCRIPTION	POST. REF.	DEBIT	CREDIT	
1							1
2							2
3							3
4							4
5							5
6							6
7							7
8							8
9							9
10							10
11							11
12							12
13							13
14							14
15							15
16							16
17							17
18							18
19							19
20							20
21							21
22							22
23							23
24							24
25							25
26							26
27							27
28							28
29							29
30							30
31							31
32							32
33							33
34							34
35							35
36							36

EXTRA FORMS

EXTRA FORMS

EXTRA FORMS